DAYS OF DRUGS AND SIRENS

MICHAEL ROMANO

Days of Drugs and Sirens

Copyright © 2012 by Michael Romano

All rights reserved. No part of this book may be reproduced or transmitted in any form or by any means, electronic or mechanical, including photocopying, recording or by any information storage and retrieval system, without the written permission of the publisher, except by a reviewer, who may quote brief passages.

ISBN-13: 978-1480218222

ISBN-10: 1480218227

DAYS OF DRUGS AND SIRENS

CONTENTS

INTRODUCTION: HOW ... WHAT ... WHY	9
1. WHEN IT ALL HITS THE FAN, WE'LL BE THERE	13
2. GIT' ALONG LITTLE DOGGIE	15
3. THE "NEVER LIE TO YOUR MOTHER, SPAGHETTI AND MEATBALL WHIPPIN'"	18
4. TROPHY FISH	21
5. WHAM BAM, THANK YOU MA'AM	25
6. YEAH, IT HURTS LIKE HELL	27
7. ALWAYS WANTED TO BE A FARMER	29
8. NEVER TOO BIG, OR TOO COLORFUL	33
9. THERE'S URBAN LEGENDS. THEN THERE'S ... UH ... WELL DONE POODLES.	37
10. NOW YOU SEE IT!	
11. PHANTOM 111 & WHO'S MYRA?	39
12. CINCO DE MAYO ALL OVER AGAIN	41
13. SAN FRANCISCO SLIP AND SLIDE	44
14. CHOKING JOLTIN' JOE	47
15. NEVER GET THE MUNCHIES ON I-5	51
16. THE BASTARD FACTORY	54
17. HOOKERS & PIMPS, AND DID I SAY LADIES OF THE EVENING? OH MY!	57
18. MOVIN' ON UP!	59
19. HOW MANY HOURS IN A WEEK?	61
20. 10/7/M ... RADIO CODE FOR MEALS	63
21. "WHAT THE HELL WERE YOU THINKING?"	66
22. CODE THREE, CODE "WHAT THE HELL?"	69
23. "I'M A 5150!"	72
24. SOMETIMES YOU JUST DON'T THINK	75
25. GHOST RIDER, I AIN'T	77
26. HOW I MET MY WIFE OR … "THE GREAT EXTORTION"	81

27. HUMOR TRUMPS DRUGS	84
28. BOOBS CAN HEAL, REALLY!	87
29. THE EXOTIC EROTIC BALL: WHAT A GREAT THING TO BEHOLD!	91
30. A CLIP OF 32 AUTOMATIC AND A HUNGRY SAMOAN STOMACH	93
31. STOP WHEN YOU HEAR THE CLICK	97
32. C.P.R., A DEAD GUY & REALLY OLD RUSSIAN LADY RACE DRIVERS	99
33. 'I GOTTA' SPLITTING HEADACHE ... AND WHAT'S THAT BUMP IN YOUR HAT?	101
34. STRAIGHT TO HELL, DO NOT PASS GO!	103
35. TO A PRIVATE MUSEUM OF AMAZING THINGS	104
36. WRONG PLACE, WRONG, WRONG TIME, WRONG SPECIES	109
37. FELONS, PEOPLE OF TRANSCENDED SEXUALITY & FEMALES	111
38. DISCRETION IS THE BETTER PART OF COMPLETELY SCREWING UP	113
39. THAT'S GOTTA BE EMBARRASSING	115
40. WHEN FAST JUST AIN'T FAST ENOUGH!	119
41. SOMETIMES IT AIN'T THE MONEY...	120
42. WHEN MEN WERE MEN AND PAIN MEANT NOTHING!	123
43. WHEN SOMEONE YELLS, "OH SHIT!" AND IS RUNNING BY YOU, FOLLOW QUICKLY AND PASS UP IF YOU CAN!	125
44. DEJA VU ALL OVER AGAIN	127
45. ONE LAST THING	131
BYE FOR AWHILE	132
DEDICATION	133
CREDITS	134

WORDS & ABBREVIATIONS
(POSSIBLY ALIEN TO YOU)

ER - Emergency Room
STICK - Start an I.V.
I.V. - A needle into the vein to run fluids
ZAP - Shock the heart/Defibrillate
SYRETTE - Sort of a itsy tooth paste tube with a needle at it's end with drug inside, disposable
CODE 3 - Lights and Sirens
CODE 2 - Lights 'No' Siren (Sort of not legal)
CODE BLUE - A Code 3, not breathing well or at all.
PIMPS - Evening entrepreneurs, of a fashion
HOOKERS - The fashion to the above mentioned
HEIMLICH MANEUVER - Rigorous back whacking and round from front to back compressions to dislodge an obstruction of the airway.
C.P.R. - Compressions of the heart while giving oxygen
RIG - An ambulance
EMPERIN - A pain pill (sometimes with Codeine, the higher the number, the more Codeine, four being pretty damn high!)
PASTIES AND G-STRINGS - Well, Look those up for yourself.
G.S.W. - Gun shot wound
P.O.S. - Piece of Sh*t
SOME RADIO CODES:
    10/7 - Out of service
    10/7m - Out for a meal
    10/49 - En Route hospital w/patient
    10/19 - Return to base
    10/97 - Arrived at scene

INTRODUCTION
HOW ... WHAT ... WHY

I spent a lot of my formative years in a Superopolis in Southern Cal. Grey skies, freeway crazies and the (way more than) occasional stray bullets. Nothing was ever easy there, but most of all, there was no 'fun!'

The faster things became, the more I knew I needed to get the hell out of that million and one horse town.

So I went to war.

It may have ended right there, but for the grace of God, and an aptitude for not throwing up when blood & guts presented themselves, I went to the North Hollywood Naval Reserve Center to enlist in the Navy, thinking, "I can't get shot on a boat."

So I took the tests, scored inhumanly high and was told to report for signing in two weeks. Sounded great and I went home feeling pretty darn secure.

At the house, a letter was waiting for me, one I figured I would never get but was happy I had already volunteered for the Navy.

You got it ... I was drafted ... and would have to report for duty with the United States Army.

I went down to the U.S.N.R.T.C. (United States Naval Reserve Training Center) the next morning smiling, and showed the commandant the letter. He frowned and said "Nothing we can do son. They have you first."

"What?" What can we do?"

"Not a darn thing" he said.

As I walked away, really feeling in the dumper, he asked, "What job did you want in the Navy?"

"Well, I've had eight years of the medical troop in boy and explorer scouts, took the sciences in high school and college. I wanted to be a Corpsman."

"What?" he said excitedly. "Come right this way!"

In I went to the Medical examiner's room, undressed, then dressed, to the swearing in room.

"Sir, what the heck is going on?"

"We need Corpsman, son."

"What about the Army?"

"I'll take care of them!"

I swore in, they shook my hand, gave me a packet of papers and told me to report to Long Beach Naval Station in two weeks.

I was bubbling and damn near danced out of the place. I had the 60's hair helmet with the long thick sideburns when I got to the gate. But not for long.

"Line up ladies, we're getting a trim."

The barber fancifully swung the sheet around my neck asking, "How would you like it?"

"Leave the sideburns," I requested.

Zip ... zip ... zoom, zoom, and I was done. Bald as a baby's hiney, except for the sideburns! I was the subject of endless ridicule and torture, but after a few days, I was allowed to shave them.

This was the first day of the rest of my life.

Bill Cosby, a great comedian and a great corpsman, once said, in a humorous attempt at describing his job in a battle zone, "The life expectancy of a Corpsman, from the time his foot touches the water, till he almost reaches the beach, is about seven seconds."

He was just being comedic. Later I'd find sometimes seven seconds was an exaggeration!

I learned what to look for in Corps school, how to really deal with it in the field. This reality check and survival technique that was imprinted on me, gave me a great knowledge to, later in my life, share and strive to be more than I had ever been before.

12   DAYS OF DRUGS AND SIRENS

ONE
'WHEN IT ALL HITS THE FAN, WE'LL BE THERE'

In the beginning - or as far back and as much as I can remember any more - there were "Ambulance Drivers." They were great in their own right but then came a new kid on the block: the "Paramedic."

Trained in the Service, as a lot of we first ones were, we were used to things being fast, crazy and as wild as could be thrown at us.

It has been said that San Francisco is a place where the circus came to town and never left! Now, this ain't a bad thing, especially if you were from a hum-drum town with constant gray skies, long freeways to anywhere and basically another war zone, to take the place of the one I had been in.

I applied to San Francisco Ambulance Company, explained what I was and the training I had and before I hung up, I was hired.

"How soon can you be here?" was his question.

"Tomorrow" was my excited answer.

Off I drove, with a suite case tied to my motorcycle and minimal money in my pocket, I was on my was the next morning at six a.m.

As soon as I got to town I was put to work that day. The Fourth of July.

Got a new rig, partner and a mission to get out there and get into the middle of it all.

Just how those words would ring true took almost 'No' time in beginning.

My new partner Troy, was a tall, well-kept, intelligent and happy chap, and allowed me to drive to our standby point to get a feel for the rig. We stopped for a libation - not what you're thinking - a 'Pepsi', and proceeded to the corner of Polk and California.

Now remember, I am from East L.A. and brand new to the Bay Area of the mid 70's. I'm also pretty fresh out of the Service where 'Don't Ask, Don't Tell' was not even on the table.

Sitting there, on the corner, all was at calm. Then, the lights came on.

There was a procession of people led by what I could only stretch my imagination to call a "Drum Major" in net stocking, lit-up platform heels, sequined G-string, festooned with an ostrich feather and fluorescent nipple covers.

Topping it all off: a spectacular headdress a la Carmen Miranda, piled high with fruit, tied in a South American Way, as Carmen would say it.

I've always thought myself capable of dealing with just about anything the universe can throw at me, and with an impressive degree of aplomb. But at this particular moment, I couldn't utter a single noise or grunt, he spoke.

"Honey, this isn't Kansas anymore," my partner smiled, awaiting my reaction.

I looked back at the passing parade, back at him and back again, as I felt a smile come to my face and started to clap out the window to the passers by.

My new partner, a kindness in his voice, said, "We'll keep you." Like an old fire horse, I was up and running!

TWO
DAYS OF MY MIND:
GIT' ALONG LITTLE DOGGIE

We got a call, one dark evening, to a very expensive neighborhood in San Francisco. A beautiful multi-level home with some lights on, but a darkened front porch.

My partner and I stopped out front, popped the gurney and equipment, and rolled to the steps up onto the darkened porch.

We knocked. Waited a moment. Heard the sounds of giggling from the other side, and looked at each other, wondering what we were in store for.

The door opens to reveal a long, dark hallway, but otherwise empty. "Hello?"

Out of nowhere, a husky voice: "Down here"

The lights came to reveal a gaggle of little people dressed in cowboy garb: the man wore a leather vest, chaps, cowboy boots (spurs included) and a ten gall-- no… make it a *three* gallon hat. Of course, this was accented by nipple rings with chains going cross and south to ... we didn't want to know.

Oh, and no pants.

The lovely little ladies were all spruced up in dance hall costumes.

We sure as hell *weren't* in Kansas anymore!

All I could think to say was "I forgot something." I spun around took the steps in two leaps, closely followed by my partner, squealing tears with his hands over his mouth.

It took five or six minutes and several bitten knuckles before we were able to regain our composure. We went back up the stairs, with as best restraint as we could come up with without medication.

Tex the wonder stud led us through the party, the gurney in tow. I must have lagged too far behind because suddenly was beset upon by a bevy of horny dance hall ladies, each no more than three and a half feet tall.

I followed the sound of the screaming - while dragging three of them down the hall on my legs - to a side bedroom. The little cowpuncher with his hands clamped onto his buttocks seemed to be ground zero.

"Well, what have we here?" It was all I could muster from my overwhelmed mind, not to mention the extra weight from my newfound admirers still hanging on.

Tex offered a hesitant explanation: "His friend was searching for ... something ... and accidentally may have ... pulled on something!"

Oh-kay. Sounds like a rectal fishing expedition and something got hooked. Not exactly what you learn in all the years of training. But I recalled one important lesson from Vietnam: if you get shot in the genitalia on the battlefield, use two Syrettes of Morphine.

Well ... this must have qualified somewhere under that rule, so POP-POP! Two onboard!

He quieted down right nicely, relaxed his nether regions, and by the time we got him to the hospital, a lot of the offending 'Bait' had retracted into it's little cubbyhole. We all piled out of the back of the rig, a smiling "lil' doggie," a couple of painted ladies, and two fairly proud medics that handled what was thrown at them.

THREE
THE "NEVER LIE TO YOUR MOTHER, SPAGHETTI AND MEATBALL WHIPPIN'"

My Mom was visiting from L.A. in my new apartment, when the question came up, "How dangerous is this line of work? I've heard things!"

It's that moment when one realizes that even though they are fully grown, and have seen combat in a foreign country, that there's still no way they can escape their Italian mother's "evil eye."

So I lied!

"Don't worry a bit, Ma. We're like a taxi but with oxygen. Yeah that's it."

Well, I get the look, a kiss on the cheek and off to work I go, on my motorcycle. And that's another bone of contention that will come up at a later time.

It's a bright morning, and we were going up Geary Blvd., approaching a huge intersection at Masonic. Suddenly, right in front of us, this little Pinto, 'P.O.S.' gets whacked broadside on the left, spun, then hit in the rear from the other direction!

We pulled over instantly. I ran towards the mess in the intersection and tried to open the driver's door.

Crushed. Jammed.

I could see a lady out behind the wheel and an infant in one of those old car seats. The kid was all wrapped up like a baby sleeping bag called a bunting, I later heard.

Smoke billowed out from under the car.

Oh, did I forget to say that there was a news reporter and a cameraman on a ride along? Paramedics were sort of a novelty still. My partner was across traffic with the gurney and I could now see a flame under the car's edge.

The edges of the bent door pooched out enough for me to fit all, what seemed fourteen fingers, over the edge. Summoning up some distant fear of fire and exploding, I yanked way more than I should have been able to. A chunking noise followed by a falling door, which allowed me to throw her over my shoulder and grab the kid like a bag of groceries!

"I was seriously younger then."

I turned around and ran several yards in what seemed an instant and there was my partner big Phil, a large man with even bigger hands ... so I pitched the baby to him, spun her in front of me as I heard a POP! POP!

This was the car really going up. In the distance, I could hear sirens, but off to my left I could see an intent little cameraman zooming in on me but the adrenaline got in the way of my caring.

That was, until he pointed to my back, which was sparkling. Some flaming particulate had landed on the ever-so-economic company windbreaker we wore, and had caught fire!

I ripped the flimsy sparkling jacket off and threw it towards the camera and just sat down. Behind me, the car spurted like the Fourth of July! It sparkled, spit and spewed flames till the Fire department slammed it out with an amazing cross blast from it's hoses.

MICHAEL ROMANO

Well, long and short of it ... the lady had bruises and a mild concussion, and the baby was fine. The Pinto was toast, burning up right there with this camera crew drooling like wild dogs and fresh meat.

After all this, you would think that this is my story. Sadly, no! I get home around 5:30, open the door to the smell of my mama's meat balls and spaghetti. After a long day, it was going to be a great dinner.

Sitting at the table, my devious mom turned the TV so that we were able to watch during dinner. You see, she had already seen the early news report and was just lying in waiting to pull the trap.

"Well Michael, anything interesting happen today?" She spoke with such a sweet voice.

"No Ma. Same old boring thing," stuffing my face with scrumptious meatballs and spaghetti.

Then in full slurp, spaghetti hanging out, there I am on the news, forty feet from a burning car in a busy intersection holding an unconscious lady in my arms, my jacket on fire.

Then, the trap slaps shut: "Is THIS what you call a safe job? One that makes you lie to your mother??!!"

Out from nowhere, came The Wooden Spoon, the same one she whomped me with as a kid! I thought, "Where the hell did she keep it hidden?" while protecting my head.

I couldn't think of anything else to do but grab my plate of spaghetti and meat balls cause she wasn't getting them back after a day like this.

Still ... where *did* she keep that spoon?

FOUR
TROPHY FISH

To preface this story ... I have always been somewhat of a shit disturber and a practical joke enabler (I'd talk someone else into doing the prank so they would get the blame).

It's 3am on a beautiful Saturday morning in the emergency room where I and a few of my classmates from Paramedic school had been stationed to learn and heal in the best of ways.

Me and my buddy were up, too much Pepsi again, and heard a screech of brakes at the emergency entrance doors. Two gentlemen came walking in, one in a bath robe barely closed in front, in a sort of a front crouch, walking in short labored steps.

I ran up, pushing a wheel chair and they both, in loud excited unison, said "OH NO!" His friend kept repeating, "Honest, he fell on it!" Now, I was aside them and could see a strange protrusion extending his bathrobe in the "rear" area.

Thinking of stories I had heard, not yet having worked in a big city as a Medic, I was fully intrigued as to what may be lodged in this most sacred of men areas.

This ER had the newest-fangled equipment money could buy. One of those things - remember that this was in the early 70s - was an exam table that could crank the top or bottom half in any direction needed.

So belly-down he went and we cranked away till his head was down, his legs were down, and the middle area was sticking up - like Everest with a flag at the summit.

The quick bets from the older nurses was leaning towards the obvious "Flashlight." I go into the doctor's lounge/sleeping quarters and try to arouse the on-duty MD and tell him of our find. Seeing it was me, and possibly remembering a few things I may have been blamed for in the recent past, he told me to leave immediately and I wouldn't die where I was standing.

I shook him again.

He glared into my eyes, saw I wasn't kidding, got to his feet and said "Lets Go," sort of like John Wayne would, if John Wayne was into freaky crap like this.

The word around the hospital spread pretty fast and we had drawn a pretty good crowd of folks awaiting the unveiling. Off comes the bath robe and - there - as in "Wild Kingdom," was the second half of what we surmised was a German Brown trout seemingly caught swimming upstream!

From preliminary math and some guessing, it was figured to be about 14 inches long, dorsal fin to tail to the part that was hiding ... a decent size trout for any fisherman!

The doc excused himself. I followed into the small empty hall behind the room, and we both had tears by now, squatting in a corner, making those snorky laugh sounds when you've passed normal laughing by a mile.

Being professionals, we regained what was left of our composure and re-entered the room, grabbing some towels on the way in so it looked like we had something to do to prepare.

Gloving way the hell up, we went in, so to speak. Tweaking and a tugging at the offending part, oh so carefully, lent to the muffled screams of our patient, as I had given him towels to bite on.

After what seemed a bit, much longer to the patient no doubt, we all came to the conclusion that, due to fins, muscles, spasms and a collective lack of fishing protocol, we were stumped.

At this point, it was about 4:00am and the senior hospital doc for whom the ER was named (you get that when you give lots of money) walked by, took a look, casually said, "Nice fish," and walked on by.

The poor guy was cleaned and prepped for a surgical room where a surgical doc would carve the fish. A young candy striper said, sort of to herself, I wonder how that could have happened?"

The old doc, passing by again, said "Great bait."

MICHAEL ROMANO

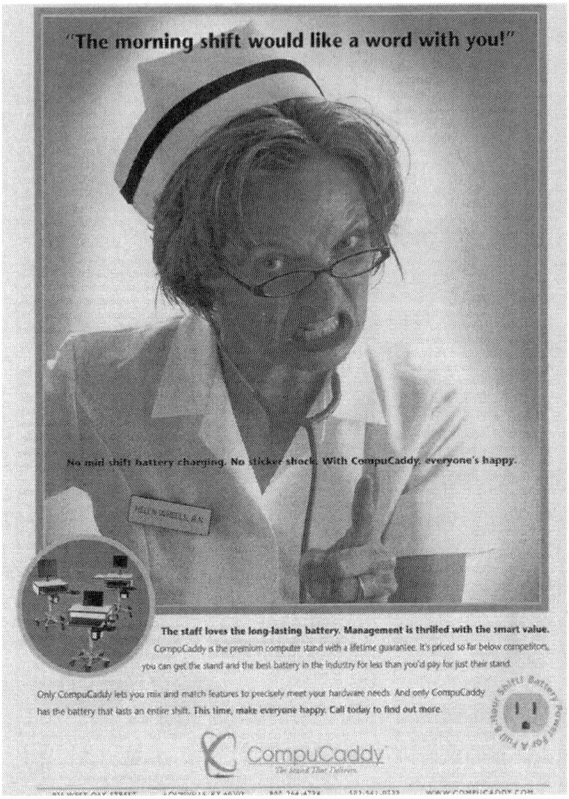
"The morning shift would like a word with you!"
No mid shift battery charging. No sticker shock. With CompuCaddy, everyone's happy.
The staff loves the long-lasting battery. Management is thrilled with the smart value.
CompuCaddy is the premium computer stand with a lifetime guarantee. It's priced so far below competitors, you can get the stand and the best battery in the industry for less than you'd pay for just their stand.
Only CompuCaddy lets you mix and match features to precisely meet your hardware needs. And only CompuCaddy has the battery that lasts an entire shift. This time, make everyone happy. Call today to find out more.
CompuCaddy
The Stand That Delivers.

FIVE
WHAM BAM, THANK YOU MA'AM

Here's a short one that could also be called *'If it lasts more than four hours, call your doctor!'*

It was Sunday morning, and I was working in another ER for the last bits of my paramedic "on the job" training. We're having the obligatory Pepsi break when a 20-year-old male gets wheeled in, curled over and groaning.

Immediately, I took two bucks on appendicitis. Daryl, whom had taken a different type of herb break, blurts out "ectopic pregnancy!" (Must have been some good stuff, but later about that!)

Into Room 1 ... we sat him on the edge of the bed and asked the starting questions, to which he said "It's been like this over a day an a half. Like this!"

They say a picture is was worth a thousand words. This wasn't worth that many, but it was pretty impressive. And there it was: a 35-hour erection!

Well, I had never had training in that end of things and couldn't remember ... well let's not go there.

We dripped cold water on it, to his painful response, sprayed it with methyl chloride, a freezy spray, at which he took a swing at me while screaming.

Finally, an old WWII nurse came in with a soup spoon and her own can of methyl chloride.

I said, "Won't work!"

MICHAEL ROMANO 25

She told me to move my ass. She then sprayed the spoon thoroughly to the confusion of the young man and then WHACKED him on the penis!

He fainted, his wheezer backed up to, I'm only guessing now, his ribcage.... and all was now right with the world. All the male medics simultaneously took one step back and covered up saying, "Ooooooooohhh" as one, um, organ!

Now with current HMO, PPO rules ... and lawyers ... this would probably not be the cure of choice today. The old nurse said, "It worked in WWII and still does, 'cuz guys were and still are all dicks! You just have to know how to handle them!"

Well, to each their own opinion.

SIX
IF YOU EVER WONDERED
... YEAH, IT HURTS LIKE HELL

This one goes way back … to school.

We were working, as part of our in-field training, at a hospital in Chino, California. Some of the rural highways were sort of elevated ten feet or so over the surrounding fields with a six foot soft shoulder (thank goodness).

Riding with existing ambulance companies seemed a pretty sure way of seeing who could handle the mess in the streets...and who would barf, wet themselves and faint.

Call goes out for a cardiac car crash. Daryl looks at me and said "Hey, a two-fer!" All excited to show our stuff, four of us piled into the first rig and away we were gone!

At the wreckage site, a car is on its side and two people are on the ground already. Two good old boys must have taken them out but we couldn't get their attention as they were trying to rock the car back on it's wheels!

No palpable pulse, Daryl and another medic started CPR, I started a line and the last guy grabbed the paddle. Oh, did I forget to say that it was misting rain?

I was on my knees by the patient just starting to push meds into a saline line (that's a steel needle in salt water connected to a wet paramedic) when I hear "CLEAR!!!"

I know I *wanted* to scream "No!" but not being faster than a bolt of lightning, it hit me! He pressed the buttons and I went up like a Roman Candle!

Next thing I knew, I was several feet away, sitting flat on my arse ... hypo still in my hand. All the hair on my right arm, armpit and right nipple were gone.

Also, sorta felt like that fat lady I picked up years later that had my arm in a scissors hold!

It took quite a few hours to be 90% again. I was placed in the shotgun seat. My partner was right there trying to bring me around with a Pepsi. My mind was a bunch thick and I wasn't quite right for a couple of hours, but I'd never pass up a Pepsi.

They told me I just smiled as we went to our next calls.

"No need to be anxious, Jeff, only 1 in 10 interns actually electrocute themselves during resuscitations, and fewer than 10 percent of those suffer life threatening arrhythmias."

SEVEN
ALWAYS WANTED TO BE A FARMER

This story is alleged to have happened as we would *never* do anything like this ...

Back in Sacramento, during the part of school when nobody had any money, when the government would give food stamps and aid to anyone, but 27 starving wannabe Paramedics couldn't get arrested, let alone financial assistance.

We'd go to the butcher and swap small cut kits for bones and meat scraps. We taught swimming at the apartment and CPR on Saturday mornings, hung over or not. We drank for free by hustling pool for snacks, drinks and cash. We'd go to the market and "acquire" three or four mushrooms, a couple of eggs each. Then we'd buy some spices and a 25-pound bag of flour, cause it was cheap and would last. I'd make beef, mushroom and dumpling soup.

Hell, to this day half of them still have dreams waking up drooling for my soup. Well enough of the morose stuff.

One day, one of my two roommates, asked me to help him look for a Tupperware box in the apartment he had misplaced. Looking under the bed, I spied a gallon plastic clear tub with little beads in it. I yelled I think I've found it.

"Yeah, there's my babies!" he said.

"What is that?" was my ignorant question.

"Those are a couple a five pounds of the sturdiest crop seeds you've ever seen!"

As the proverb goes, "Give a man a fish and he'll eat for a day. Teach him to fish and he'll eat for a lifetime."

Thus, I embarked on my lifelong ambition to plant! Especially in empty lots out of town, near creeks. Spots that were in plain sight but no one cared to look there … and they even make beautiful houseplants that can be made to flourish and yield o' plenty.

Now *selling* of such a thing may be construed as incorrect, even illegal. But *trading* seemed not only natural but downright easy! Gasoline, rent, food, clothes … you name it, and the 70's had it! Even platform shoes!

School and horticulture pretty well took up all waking moments. We needed a much agreed-upon diversion. We took a Saturday morning off from swimming and CPR classes, and went on a tour of the capitol building, making note of the beautiful grounds and hedges all through it. A herd of little old Japanese Gardeners did miracles with the grounds.

I looked to him, then towards the bushes. "They'd blend right in planted neatly, wouldn't they?" The next week went by like a shot, planning and drawing our masterpiece for the government.

Late Friday, we pulled up on the cycle with two long spades and two plastic bags of seeds. Behind either side row of hedges, we made a long dig in the dirt from front to back, sowing seeds the whole length.

Then, on the way out, covered them up. We waited for the automatic sprinklers and the gardeners to either yank them out or tend them thinking they were a new back plant or something. It didn't really matter if it worked, we had done it! And that was enough.

Months later, we were driving by the Capitol building. There were dozens of guys in black suits, the area was yellow-taped off and two small flatbed trucks were on the lawn area.

As we saw on the news that night, the gardeners did such a good job that our bush, being fed so well, watered every day and curried like a prize horse, grew into a hedge, of sorts! Those guys were plucking plants and interrogating the gardeners. My roomie just looked at me and said, "Yeah. Whew!"

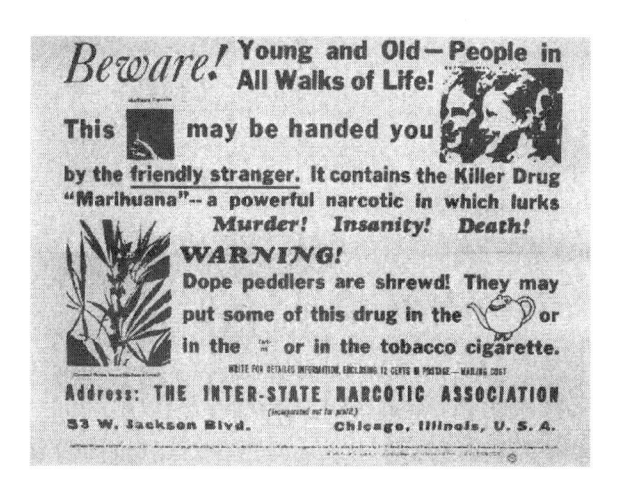

MICHAEL ROMANO

EIGHT
NEVER TOO BIG, OR TOO COLORFUL

Working into my third straight 24-hour shift, we pulled back into headquarters for a well-deserved collapse and my driver piles out, the back door opens, the crew re-fits the rig in two minutes. While I'm sitting there, popping the top on a Pepsi, a new driver hops in, hits the lights and siren and takes off like a shot.

"I'm waaayyy off right now! Take me back!"

"Got a code three! And she's a big one!"

Well, I'm a big strapping Italian boy and my new partner is somewhere near 5-foot-tall, wearing a T-shirt under her open uniform top (she just woke up and was not completely put together) On this T-shirt were two petite fried eggs where breasts on a girl who weighed over 85 pounds would have had them!

We get to the address, and it's up 45 stairs, three feet wide, carved out of the rocky hill. A beautiful vista, if the patient was not the retired tattooed, Fat Lady from a circus.

Dragging up all the gear, and we found out quickly: Not enough stuff! Up that flight to heaven, we entered a nice home with a picturesque view and large posters of a ginormous lady all covered in tattoos!

She yelled from the bathroom where she had fallen and broken her femur (the long bone in the thigh). This is a very dangerous break as if it cut the femoral artery, she could bleed out lickety split.

But we had the right tool: a hare traction splint. We stretch and lock the leg in a safe position. Aha, we're ready ...

Maneuvering around the half-jammed door, I saw a little bit more of her than I wanted to, caught myself staring and looked away. She screamed "pervert!" Hardly. In fact, if I'd ever thought of turning gay, this was it!

The best way to describe her would be to say that she used to be fully-painted 675-pounds, but now weighed in at a much-slimmer 400-pounds, but with the same amount of skin!

I didn't realize it was possible to apply a splint while being bludgeoned by wild fists from a still-sturdy lady, but sometime I surprise myself.

After the beating, she tried to cover herself with a bath towel, hurling other slurs and invectives toward me as my partner left to use the phone. When my partner failed to return immediately, I went to investigate, but had to finally admonish the patient, who hadn't slowed her actions or her mouth.

MICHAEL ROMANO

"STOP moving!"

My pard had called the Fire Brigade from the nearest station just blocks away. Thank God there were some beefers among them, cause my driver was only good for moral support and the occasional "Jeezus!"

Getting the patient onto the gurney all at once was a mathematical impossibility. Trying grab hold as her skin flailed in many directions threw us. And all the time yelling, oddly only at me.

"Did you get a good feel??? Sicko!"

We rocked her back and forth carefully onto a blanket and when we had her (or most of her) centered, we all lifted, and placed her atop the gurney, making sure to cover and tuck her under, as much as humanly possible.

Then it struck me - Oh my God - the stairs ...

Why we went feet first and I was alone on the bottom, I never found out. But she slid towards me, allowing two things to happen.

To put this kindly ... her boobs, not as full as they once were, but having plenty o' skin, flopped out from under the blanket onto my left hand, completely ruining any desire to date anyone for the next month. With one hand share holding up the bottom, one hand holding side for stabilization to even out the load.

And what a load.

She also now figured out how to elevate the long metal splint, although I didn't know how. And slam it down onto my shoulder, screaming in a language I could only believe was Gypsy, because of the evil eye horns she was giving me with her free hand!

Mercifully, we got to the bottom before she had beaten me unconscious and as I would fall, run me over. We locked her gurney into the ambulance and I stuffed an oxygen mask onto her to slow down what I could only believe were Gypsy Curses. I told my driver to go now, "Code 3!"

It was the end to a very long day. I walked out of the ER, sat down on the curb, took a sip of you-know-what, and looked up. A fetching nurse slowly approached and asked if I'd had a full night.

I said, "You could easily say that."

Whereupon she said with a smile, "Would you like to make it fuller?"

I scratched my eyebrow and looked crooked up to her and said, "Take a look in room one. I just brought her naked, down the side of a tall hill half on my shoulders with things flopping everywhere. I just don't think I'm gonna for awhile."

She patted me on the head and said, "God owes you one." I could only work up a thankful smile but hers was big enough for the both of us…

(To understand this last line, put yourself doing something good, where no one else will ever know but you, God, and that smiling nurse.... love, dad.)

"Works great with bacon, potatoes, and ... poodles!"

NINE
THERE'S URBAN LEGENDS. THEN, THERE'S ... UH ... WELL DONE POODLES.

Got a call one day for a code cardiac. Lights and sirens make us hoot and holler, especially since I learned how to make the new electronic siren yelp, squeal, howl and ... yes ... even Bark!

I flew down Van Ness yelling over the loud speaker "PULL OVER TO THE RIGHT! NO, YOUR OTHER RIGHT!"

Well, too soon, we're there. Up stairs and stairs and stairs to her apartment to find her sitting on the floor of her kitchen in a pool of what wasn't chardonnay. She is holding her chest and asks, "How's my baby?"

We scan the place and find this enormous microwave. You see, the old-time ones were so antiquated that a two-and-a-half foot cube of a microwave only had about enough room for a TV dinner. On the front was a rather obvious metal plaque that read "Don't use if you have a pacemaker."

That's when we noticed a curly-haired critter leg sticking out. The smell of Ben Gay wafting through the air had masked the perfume of Poodle au Microwave.

She again asks, "How is my baby?"

Big Phil, thinking some humor might put things right says, "Well Done!"

Well...she 'infarcts' (full on heart attack), slumped over, and dropped like a rock. Phil popped her chest to no avail, then starts CPR and bagging, as I get the paddles. Open the shirt place the paddles and - BAM - she goes right back into an acceptable rhythm.

While I'm starting a line, I told Phil to ditch the dog. I don't know if he was a religious man but I heard him call God and Jesus a lot as he tried to pick up the cooked teacup poodle, as I was to later find out, with an oven mitt and a two-pronged turkey fork he found in a drawer, out the window it went.

She has now become more aware and asks one last time about her little darling. "I put him in there to dry. Is he alright?"

I looked at Phil with that "shut the hell up" stare I learned from watching my mom give it to my dad at Christmas parties. I told the little old lady that her baby went on the first ambulance and should be just fine!

Phil whispered to me, "what's gonna happen when she finds out?" I told him it's our job to get her there pink and perky and that I personally knew the on duty nurse was a dog lover and would find the words.

So, when you hear an urban legend and wonder if it is or it ain't, take a word from Phantom 111 and go, "Hmm ... maybe ..."

TEN
NOW YOU SEE IT!

Having been from East L.A., I hadn't been exposed to a lot of things, other than gang fights, foreign countries and war ... but that was nothing compared to the new and wildly exciting San Francisco.

I was working for a fledgling private ambulance company. As a matter of fact, my first shift started forty-five minutes after arriving at the company during the same hour I hit town!

A week later, not long after Halloween, we get a call for a possible overdose. Code three and a Pepsi was called for, so we amped up en route (we had a small indispensable ice chest with the elixir close at hand).

We arrived with lightening speed and a possible, as I recollect, speed-wedgie. We flew up the stairs to find a very clean-looking female - long blond hair, ample breasts, and all-spiffed nails, etc. - in a short nightgown, unconscious on the floor.

Cleared the airway, started CPR, got her down the three stairs and into the ambulance so fast, I even impressed myself. I started a line and push a drug called Narcan. This blocks 'Opiates' at their beginning. Suddenly, she gasped, spitting out the airway, and began to breathe on her own.

I Got online to the hospital to ask directions. The doc wanted me to draw blood to check for how much opiates were in her system. After doing so, I proceeded to report progress to central as we were close.

Well, we wore these bulky headsets with this arm-like speaker coming around all the way to your mouth. Not like the wireless sticks they have today.

The ride was bumpy so I pulled the blanket up to cover her shortie pajamas. At the same time, we hit a pothole that produced a rearward snap ... Out from under the ruffly cloth flang a very large organ she was *not* supposed to have!

Having never been exposed to this type of dual transmission before, I jumped back, stabbed myself in the thigh with the needle and said some unintelligible profanities directly into the microphone!

It took a moment for me to semi-regain my remaining composure and do my job and put a cold pack on the injection site. That's when "she" woke up. "WHAT Are you doing?"

I tried to explain, quickly, why I had her nether regions flapping in the wind and was somewhat successful in keeping her calm.

Getting to the ER door, we sped her in. The nurses took her and I pulled the doc over, explaining what happened. He said, "Both?"

"Yep," I responded.

He said, "Neat!" and closed the door behind him.

Well, just like the Lone Ranger, we rode off into the sunset, or more close to evening, all that mattered was that "she" was fine. Not forgotten though.

I became known as the "AC/DC paramedic," a reputation that traveled from hospital to hospital till something new took it's place.

Oh, and they did!

ELEVEN
PHANTOM 111 & WHO'S MYRA?

My best partner and main tormentee Little Phil, was my best friend and ambulance roomie, as we lived in that damnable vehicle three times longer than we were off. Oh, and we lived in the same apartments next door to each other too.

We were called the crew of "Phantom 111" for the supernatural reason as to where ever we got a call to, either we got there in unnatural time, all from dead reckoning by the compass...or turned a block and were right there! Central would amaze, saying "Already?" No answer on our part, just up and out to the call.

One cold crisp day, I talked Phil into letting me drive the rig, a brand new behemoth of a modern ambulance slash hot rod that had just arrived. Immediately, he had second thoughts about letting me behind the wheel of so much engine and iron on the hoof! I said, "What could possibly happen?"

Tooling around town, revving up the motor when we came next to other ambulance companies seemed to be the limits of my driving exploits with "Phantom 111" as we called her ... or so Phil believed.

MICHAEL ROMANO

"Code 3," came over the radio and Phil immediately said "Okay, let's swap seats."

"Too Late!" I replied with a squeal of glee and punched the pedal, lifting the whole new rig up as the dual carburetors both kicked in! Barely in control, zooming down upper Market Street towards our destination, Phil was clamped onto the dashboard like an abalone to a rock.

There was a shortcut, I believed, on 17th Street, which had a cable car line on it. In the distance, I could see one or those old 40's pig iron trolleys coming toward us, as by now I was on the wrong side of the street, sirens blaring, trying to pass the cars on the right who wouldn't pull over to let me by.

Phil's grasp tightened. Still no comment from him.

As the trolley got closer, I sped up to pass the car to the right but he was having none of that and he sped up! Closer and by now speeding pretty fast, Phil was rigid, not squirming at all anymore.

The SOB in the other car must not have known that I had a 440 cubic inch engine with a double-pumper carburetor under the hood cause when I punched the gas and swerved to the right in front of him - missing the trolley by a breath. He looked at me: half in amazement and half, what I'd like to believe, envy. I glared, grinned at him and sped on.

A heartbeat later, Phil shouted, "MYRA!"

Just around the block was the address. We screeched to a stop, jumped out, did our thing, all was well and we were off (some kind of self-induced senility disallows me to remember what the heck kind of a call it was) but I do remember what happened next.

As we drove away, Phil seemed to be in a trance.

I looked over to him and asked, "Phil, who the hell is Myra?"

He looked directly into my eyes and said "My third grade sweetheart! My whole life flashed before me!"

I told him it was O.K. and to be glad he wasn't Italian or the show would still be going on. He said, "Let's get some BBQ and a Pepsi."

My thoughts exactly.

He even forgot to change places with me till the shock wore off.

TWELVE
CINCO DE MAYO ALL OVER AGAIN

A pretty good time is had by all in the Latin districts of San Francisco. And I emphasize pretty darn good! Food, a Festival in every section of town, much laughter, and ... the drinks!

In the gringo community, Super Bowl Sunday puts the beer companies immediately into the black. But Cinco de Mayo beats them all. Between beer and tequila, I never saw as many full on grins as on that day.

Well, here's the story: we got a silent code three (not too legal to run the lights without the sirens but told to do so as not to excite the block parties). We get to a taped-off block, being led in by three apparently hammered individuals, each with a different version of what was going on.

Down to mid block, there was a '55 Chevy with no front tires down on the asphalt, on it's drums. Being on the left side, coming up on the front of the car, I could see a pair of feet and legs coming into view. Then full around to the front and - VIOLA - a party reveler laying under the front of the bumper.

Partier number one said he had been working on the bottom of his radiator, when somehow, unknown to anyone there, the Christmas Tree jack stands popped out, allowing the chrome bumper to fall forward onto this now very agitated man's forehead.

The drums kept the car from crushing his head like the large piñata stretched on a rope across the street but pinned him there fast to the ground.

Seeing that this situation could do with a little planning, my partner and I backed up a bit away from the drunken three's constant suggestions.

Then a scream came from the front of the car and we ran back to witness two of the crowd getting instructions on how to yank our patient out by each lifting a leg into the air and pulling.

This did *not* free him but *did* succeed in partially scalping him as the bumper and the pulling cut the forehead skin line clean and straight.

So bizarre was this scene, it took me a full 15 seconds before I shouted "Alto! (stop)," and they did right away, still holding his legs in the air.

I noticed a good-sized floor jack 30 feet up his driveway, and motioned for some help. Before long, the partiers got the jack, and pumped up the car.

Before we pulled him, we pulled his hairline back down, wiped it off and taped it. His comrades smiled, patted him on the back, gave him a beer and cheered!

Then everyone cheered!

Our patient seemed to like the adulation and got right into the ambulance, waving to the crowd like a football hero, beer and all, off to the hospital with a hell of story for next Cinco de Mayo to tell to his children.

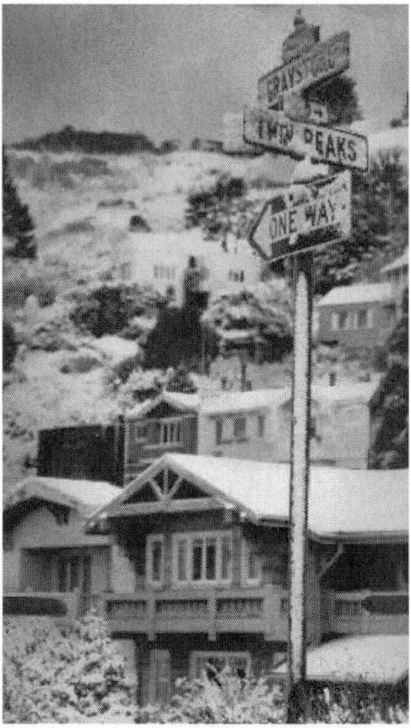
TWIN PEAKS
ONE WAY

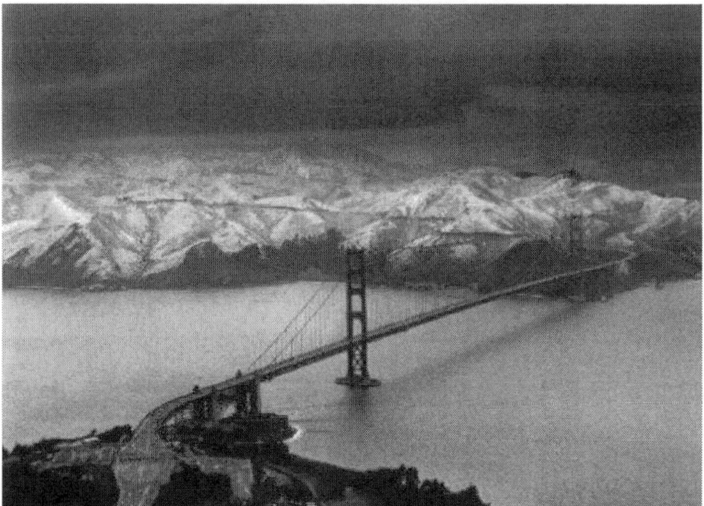

THIRTEEN
SAN FRANCISCO SLIP AND SLIDE

Sitting in my ambulance, one morning, it started to snow in San Francisco. I only had a couple of hours left to my 100-hour shift (only slightly kidding) and I'm just fishing for a little sympathy, so Control told us to stand by at the "Top of the Hill," up by my future wife Joanne's home, near Upper Market where it turns into Portola.

We started toward there, but when we got to the bottom of the hill and started to go up, the wheels began to spin on the icy, snowy ground. I told my partner to pull into the gas station and face the rig towards "up the hill."

What ensued was better than drunks ice skating! Cars going up the hill got 200 feet or so up, and came right back down! Straight, angled, sideways and so on.

Newcomers to the hill couldn't possibly miss the pile up of cars at the bottom, but proceeded to drive around them and try for themselves. We began to laugh so hard that I had to ask the gas station attendant for the key to the important room.

When I got out, the police had arrived, stopping the flow of traffic upwards and keeping the, now, crowd from shouting obscenities at each other.

All seemed well until - on the other side of the mid-barrier - a downhill car shot through at a 45 degree angle, which made us commence to giggling again. Here came a couple more, like beginners on the ice, doing all kinds different twists and slides.

For just a moment, we had an idea to try and prevent this carnival on ice. Then, we came to our senses, called it in to dispatch to send police and tow trucks.

We had eight or nine cars clustered at the bottom all snug up against each other, and now at least that many in and through the intersection coming down. We made an attempt to see if anyone was injured ... luckily no.

Just lots of body and fender work and a passel of pissed off people!

I went off duty, picked up Joanne down the hill at her work and we went to the park and threw snowballs for the first time anyone had done that, in San Francisco since I was born in 1949.

Still have the picture someone took of us in the park in the snow…pretty neat.

FOURTEEN
CHOKING JOLTIN' JOE

Another alleged happening, as perhaps the statute of limitations ain't up. Money was hard to come by, and $3.48 an hour for all the hours you could stay awake didn't pile up, even when you slept sitting up in your seat (or not at all).

So, one needed to be a little more than a bit creative. Going to restaurants and offering to set up a great cut and burn kit for employees and keep it restocked, also teach the cooks, waiters and waitresses the Heimlich Maneuver seemed a fair trade for three dinners for the two of us ... and maybe a couple of lunches.

The manager told me to "Cop a Walk!" and get out.

As the gods of hunger were on our side, a portly gentleman sitting at a center table, began to choke, turn a lovely shade of violet and show the surrounding customers why not to eat there.

Looking at the choker, then at the manager, I then smiled, nodding my head towards the large purple man to my immediate left.

He yelped, "Yes!"

Just one word uttered and I had the guy up, thumping on his back and doing my best to reach around him for the big yank on his diaphragm. That's just above the belly and below front rib cage.

Whump! Whump! And a piece of beef the size of a small child shot out, hit the table, and off to the floor, where a waiter quickly picked it up, cleared the table and (taking a hint from the manager) immediately carried the man into the office where my partner had already set up an oxygen mask to gas him back up to par. The manager said "Three dinners, three lunches!"

I smiled, nodded my head and that would have been a good enough story, but ... as we were walking out, a tall well-dressed older man in the corner beckoned to me.

Being done, I walked a few steps and stopped.

He asked me, "Do you know who I am?"

Quietly, I answered. "Everyone knows who you are, Mister DiMaggio."

He was writing on a napkin, and handed it to me. It read "Good job, and signed it 'Joe DiMaggio.'

I tipped my hat and he put his two fingers to his brow then we parted ways, off to serve and protect, and to hustle up a few more goodies before the night was through.

FIFTEEN
NEVER GET THE MUNCHIES ON I-5

My Paramedic School partner, roommate and best buddy and I had driven to Los Angeles, for some forgotten reason, in my 1972 Honda 600 sedan. A superb specimen of a car with a 600cc two-piston motorcycle motor that I had souped-up to almost 95 horse power!

Don't scoff ... it was a hottie!

My 10-inch tall radials had been beefed up to a wider tire, never mind where they came from, but with all that horse power and meat tires, my mighty mini car would scoot and hug a corner like a scalded cat!

On the way back to Sacramento to our school, Darryl decided to stuff some of his mystical home grown mind-melt into a contraption he called a "Shotgun Carburetor."

An interesting enough item, pretty complex but not something to bring fear into my heart.

"You see," he said, "You fill the filter chamber with stuff, then ball some up, roll it into the bowl, light the Zippo, put your finger over the end hole, three puffs on the tube and let go your finger on the fourth."

I followed directions like a good student. Roll, stuff, light. Finger, finger, finger, and Whooooosshh!

Jesus! I felt like I was force-fed a burning shed as my eyes rolled back. "Hey, Darryl! Yeah!" One more for me and the extra contact high I got from his *eleven* hits, and ... yeah. I was wasted, but functioning, although at 28 miles an hour in the slow lane on the freeway coming north from L.A. towards Sacramento. About 20 minutes later, the subject of food came up.

Darryl said, "Next off-ramp is a road side rest (a restaurant)! This was a good thing as, I surely had a new found hunger that had no sense, just direction.

As were pulling into the parking lot at Mach Nothing, he says "One more hit, cause it's good for digestion."

At this point, this seemed a feasible and correct thought pattern so I leaned over towards the center of the seats as we creeped into the parking stall.

He yelled "Stop," so I hit the brakes, and set the emergency. Then, Darryl leans over with that evil smirk of his, and says "Look on both sides of us."

There were two highway patrol cruisers neatly caressing our parking space. I thought I soiled myself. I glared at my buddy, who was having too much fun to be my good friend at that moment and asked "What do we do?"

"Let's get somethin' to eat and the world will look better."

"Really?" I slurred. "Yep, really," was the last thing I remember till I sat down in these booths with two foot tall swirley orange plastic booth separators.

"Nobody can see ya, buddy" were very soothing words.

"Except maybe them." He gestured, slowly looking over the edge on either side.

I didn't want to, but some primitive urge of self protection and sheer gross stupidity, not to forget being severely hammered, coaxed me to look. Two large, starched uniformed, gun-and-club-carrying cops on both sides of me just gave me a glare as I smoothly slid down onto the fine vinyl of the bench seat.

The ass who was my friend was silently giggling and about to order. To this day I remember saying "I take the same" have no clue what I ate.

But it was good, I recall.

Time to leave. Up again I scooched to check out the surrounding area. Both still there. And I got that same glare through those mirrored pilot's glasses.

Must have left a great tip cause I remember the waitress saying, "Hey, thanks boys!"

Darryl got up first and said "C'mon." I stood up, looking straight ahead, thinking "No one knows."

Then one of the cops said to us, "If he can't handle it..." That's all I heard as we made a quick but not freaky exit to the car.

Darryl drove the rest of the way, I believe. We made it back to Sacramento and that was the last time I ever did that. Well, at least to that extent. While driving. And around policemen.

Well enough said about that possible occurrence.
Just another day of school and the wonders of all the things that were to come, that would open my eyes, forever!

SIXTEEN
THE BASTARD FACTORY

There was a place in the city for unwed young mothers which we, perhaps unkindly, dubbed "The Bastard Factory." A Christian-run group that wore certain black vestments, ran this establishment (I will not get them angry with me by naming any folks directly, as I still fear them from when I had them as teachers in school).

But needless to say, that when the call came for a delivery, it was at the last moment and invariably 3:00 in the morning. Oh, yes. A screaming teenager with a Matron in tow (the aforementioned ladies in black-tented attire), screaming orders to us about what to do, of which they had no idea.

Getting the young lady in the back of my ambulance with her companion, was interesting, as we were told in no uncertain terms not to touch her in any un-lady-like fashion or look at any private parts.

Well, figuring this had already been done, to some level or another, I needed to figure how to get rid of the excess baggage.

While under way, this time, I asked the Plus One if she would kindly go through the door, separating the cab in front from my rear work area and grab my non existent medical bag .

Getting her balance, she stumbled into the cab, where I gave her a little shove and locked the door behind her. She then commenced to verbally (and a bit physically) to my surprise and a little bit of giggling on my part, turn on my partner.

Threats of everything from jail to hell came out of that little lady, not forgetting the shaking in anger of a rosary at my poor cowering driver/ buddy/ scapegoat.

Now to the matter at hand, a large-tummied, screaming girl who was - let me take a look - ah, yes ... crowning!

That means that the top-most part of the baby's head was now visible. With my young mother-to-be in position, I prepared for delivery 'en route.'

My partner's companion, up front, could see all this, as well as my looking under the sheet at her nether regions. I think my (soon to not want to be my) partner got some religion that night, praying for no traffic as to arrive at the hospital as soon as possible.

By the time we reached the ER, mom and baby were hugging, the Matron was fairly impressed with us and our work, and she even gave me a knuckles in the arm like an 'attaboy.'

Well, I'd like to think it was that and not a punch.

The hospital doctors were waiting outside for us and took great charge to care for the new mom and child.

In parting, the new mom's keeper turned to me and asked my name, I said, "Michael, but please, I have kids all over the world named after me." She sort of squinted

MICHAEL ROMANO

one eye and glared. "No, No! Not for that. I just have delivered many babies in some amazing places."

She smiled (sort of) and said that she asked for my name, not for the mom, but to be added in her prayers. She added, "Someone best be prayin' for ya'!"

She then turned, following the procession of doctors and nurses with her rosary in hand, hopefully praying for my salvation ... not for what she was saying in the ambulance on the way.

SEVENTEEN
HOOKERS & PIMPS, AND DID I SAY LADIES OF THE EVENING? OH MY!

The "Tenderloin" of San Francisco is a true wonder of the modern age of the creative entrepreneur. From knockoff tennies and high-end ten dollar watches (three for $25), my regular shift from 11:00 pm to 7:00 am (which could easily end up being to the next night) was nothing if not an education in the real world on steroids.

I had heard the statement of the description of San Francisco as the "town where the circus came and never left!" I found this was far from the truth. More so, everywhere else was Kansas, and this was OZ!

Around every corner lay a new secret, ready to show itself to me, and I could hardly contain myself, waiting for them. As I said before, money was not always readily incoming, and here starts a tale.

I knew many people in oft times, considered to be, "low places." As to their occupations, well, this may have been true. Ladies and gentlemen of the evening, who were sometimes posing as the other, were quite concerned about their health, which could change from week to week.

The major unseen culprit, of the time, was a disorder commonly known as "the Clap." Please excuse my wordage, but the other name is much worse.

Knowing how to test for this, I embarked on a mission to check and help these folks as best I could.

Setting up a morning, once a week, I would do the necessary check-ups. A mild remuneration was involved, to offset the costs, and a small cottage industry had been established. Word of mouth was pretty good and so was business.

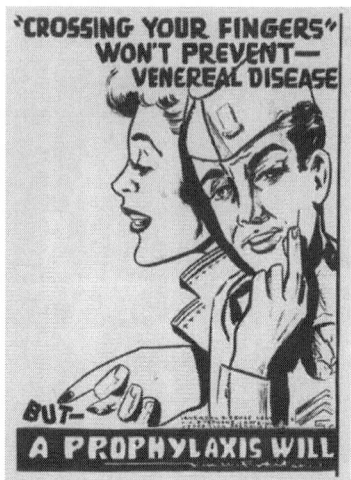

At ten dollars a pop, I had a steady weekend clientele.

With the knowledge, and a few extra dollars they were able to get proper treatment, so as not to interrupt their evening jobs too much.

Sharing, of sorts, would give one a bad name in the business and even less referrals, if you know what I mean....and if you don't, well then, you are a better person than I am.

EIGHTEEN
MOVIN' ON UP!

Making more, as I worked ungodly hours, I was able to afford a stunning apartment at the "Top of the Hill, San Francisco." A veritable penthouse with views to die for.

Having spent every available penny on this place, my funds (or rather, the lack of) did not have a single dollar factored in towards furniture.

This is where my level of hustle automatically kicks in all on it's own and really shines. "Furniture is no more than cloth and stuffing."

This is the premise my mind grabbed on to. First the stuffing. Pillows, where could I get pillows?

Putting out the call, to my fellow broke buddies, in return for a promise of a dinner of my momma's Meatballs and spaghetti with that super sauce of hers, the great pillow hunt was on.

Over the next week, my companions, fellow workers and friends, began dropping off pillows to my apartment. I never asked where they came from, as I know all my friends were upstanding folks.

Although some were mysteriously stamped with institutional names, hmmm, go figure?

Next phase, the skin to mold and hold these fluffy stuffings. San Francisco basically has anything you can conjure up, from the normal to the most bizarre mind, as mine would go off into and play by itself.

Downtown, there were some shops of, shall we say, of questionable work ethic, and needed someone to set up and train workers to treat minor cuts and bruises with a well stocked kit.

Viola! Corduroy by the roll. It was a cool fashion statement for 'Corduroy Suits' in the mid 70's. No, really! Sewing the shapes was none too hard, then stuffing was a snap.

Again, Viola! A 10-foot couch of larger than life proportions: comfortable, and two plush chairs to match. Liberating a large wooden spool, similar to the ones some folks may use for telephone wire, got sanded, verithained, and a coffee table was born!

Lamps from here and there were re-painted and what my old partner said as he walked in, "Well, I'll be goin' to hell!"

A proper bachelor pad has been given birth to.

I truly loved that place. A far cry from the paid-by-the-week room-and-board hundred-shared hotel room I started with. I also had "wheels." Well, two of them, in the form of a motorcycle. I guess I was living "the Vida Loca," way before the song came out!

The spaghetti and meatball dinner promised to everybody, turned out to be a great party, in my new furnished pad at top of the world.

<u>NINETEEN</u>
HOW MANY HOURS IN A WEEK?

Our pay was straight time: no extra for overtime ... At least that's the way my paycheck and I remember it.
Paramedics were few and far between. The call for them meant higher premiums for an ambulance ride as we had much more training than any one else out there.

"Hey Mike, wanna work a double?" That's the way it always started, but that double would become a "triple," which turned into taking cat naps between calls and stopping to grab food and "get rid of it!"

Personal time became exactly that, between changing rigs for a re-stocked one, get a new driver, a quick poop ... and the holy of holies, Pepsi, to start the engines and out again to save mom, apple pie and the occasional 'What the hell is This!'

The gamut of gunshots to cardiac, from 50 cats in an old ladies home to little folks in leather and chains, nothing deterred us from the path.

Although, sometimes the path got a bit blurry with lack of down time, whenever we hit a scene, the adrenalin that is only reserved for youth took completely over, with a turbo from a strategically placed Pepsi, and I was so alert as to amaze those around me.

This week went through like a never ending beating: Full on ... nap ... pumping in high gear, eat, nap, wash, rinse, repeat.

Next thing I remember was being back in the station and somebody saying "Payday."

Payday! Now let's see how we did.

First, the hours: 142. It seemed not to register. I walked down to the office and asked to use one of those old time calculators. Let's see: 24 hours times 7 days equals 168 hours in a week. How the hell did I work that many?

A couple of my drivers were there and said, "Oh yeah, Mike. You were in the rig forever that week. I got out to get your food so you could catch a nap and eat on the way to a call. You were there alright."

"Thought you died a couple of times but when the call came..."

My partner drove me home and I slept for the better part of a whole day.

I'll leave this one with this: it took years before I could have a phone ring while I was asleep not to jump straight out of bed, get my pants on and look around for my driver to have instructions, and if you don't believe me ... ask my wife!

TWENTY
10/7/M ... RADIO CODE FOR MEALS

Our favorite code.

Rest, Food, Pepsi and down time for the brain. Even though their duration stretched from half an hour to on the run!

During the first weeks of my new San Francisco life, I found that the eating establishments in the town far surpassed anything I was used to before. Greek, Chinese and good ol' fashioned Southern Bar-BQ all co-existed side by side. Oh, the wonder of it all!

This was the beginning of so many new and ever surprising countries of delicacies that awaited me. One evening, as a matter of fact, dinner time, nothing was going on and all was at peace in the City. My partner said, "I bet you've never had 'Real Chinese' cooking."

Having come from a town with very few Chinese folks and only 'Wong's Paradise' which served what non-Chinese folks called Original Chinese Cuisine.

My partner said, "Just as I figured. I'm taking you to my special, 'No Whites in Sight' Hunan restaurant."

"Chinese, huh?" I questioned ignorantly.

"Oh Yeah...you are gonna be amazed!"

We parked in the red zone out front. I looked at the curb, pointed down to it and was told to shut up and breathe. Not even in the door and I was leaving drool pools wherever I stopped.

"Look at the menu," he commanded "and see if you recognize anything from home."

Not a damn thing and I didn't care, as the aromas were right from God's dining room.

"Hey, here's one sounds great." Well it had four stars, like in my mom's old TV Guide, which meant excellent. "Mongolian Beef." Man, did that sound adventurous!

The plate came...all $3.65 of it.

I already knew how to use chopsticks as well as anyone, grabbed a ton, then got a 'Code 3' on the radio.

I looked up at my driver, then down at my plate. $3.65 and all that smell is going to come with me at least in part. Sucking what had to be almost half the plate, even the waiter looked shocked at me.

Thinking that he'd never seen a large Italian gorge himself ... or .... the four stars on the menu didn't mean great. It meant Nuclear! He took off towards the kitchen, I started to hear noises in my ears and dropped to one knee leaning over a stool.

Couldn't talk as I was busy trying to breathe and splash water in my mouth. My eyes were rapidly drying out. Here came the waiter, flying out of the kitchen with what looked like milk.

"Don't swallow! Swish! Spit!"

He held a bucket in front of me.

It tasted funny but it was working.

God, I hoped that was milk.

All this time, my driver told Central Station that I was doubled over a chair in China Town and to send another rig.

Thank goodness it turned out to be a crank call.

I found out two things that day. The care and procedure for an idiot in a Hunan Chinese restaurant, and 'Screw the TV Guide!'

TWENTY-ONE
"WHAT THE HELL WERE YOU THINKING?"

Many small things filled the days. All weren't epic saves or dangerous adventures, but some gave pause to scratch my head. One night when I was running a local 'Emergency Room' in the outer mission, a mother bought her six-or-so-year-old boy in with a bandage on his face, all covered in blood.

This got me up from behind my desk and snapped to so I could get my proverbial teeth into something other than paperwork. Almost salivating as I unwrapped his face (sorta sick, I know) but at that time I was a fix-it junkie.

Protruding from his blood faucet of a nose was, a 4-inch threaded bolt with a nut on the end, stuck way up in his nose. Mom had been trying to pull if out of her son's screaming bleeding face for the better part of an hour before she brought him in, with ... two aunts, Nana, a pair of sisters and some neighbor to be named later.

Everyone had an opinion which almost immediately turned into a heated argument. I needed a minute in silence, so I grabbed the kid and pulled him, unnoticed if you can believe it, into a side room.

I said "You're gonna be fine with nobody else yanking at you. Just be calm and trust me."

Putting one finger on the top side of his nose, where the nut was stuck. I locked onto the bolt with a 'straight mosquito,' a small uncurved hemostat, which is sort of a long skinny pair of pliers with a grabber lock.

Gently screwing counter clockwise, I quickly freed the bolt just as Mama and her gang burst into the room.

Surprised, they stared at the bloody bolt on the tray as I leaned the boy slightly forward tapping above the nut jam spot atop his nose, it, with a little help, tumbled right out.

I cleaned him up to the symphony of ladies saying to each other that, that is precisely what they would have done if the others would have shut up and let them "think." When it was over, I gently tapped the kid on his head and smiled.

He looked at the gaggle of ladies, then to me ... shook his head slowly, and walked out. Yep, another amazing save was over. And who is that at the front desk?

Ah yes, a young lady with an ear hole stuffed with sunflower seeds that her mom tried to get out with a water pick, swelling them up twice their size.

"Next Contestant!"

TWENTY-TWO
CODE THREE, CODE "WHAT THE HELL?"

One night in the Bayview district, we - me and a new guy named John - ran on a call of a beating. Why we were called instead of police didn't matter as it was a dull night and we were up for all of it.

Getting to a wide intersection, under a tall, fairly bright street light, we saw a few young men in long white T-shirts grouped together leaning and looking, sort of, around the corner.

We just caught the sight of a slight-sized man chasing a rather full bodied lady with an ice pick, jabbing at her repeatedly.

Then ... silence.

I looked at the guy at the front of the T-shirt group, which was, by this time, growing and he looked at me ... for a split second, before the couple came back around the corner again ... this time with *him* being chased by *her* as she flailed a blonde wood-colored furniture table leg sort of in a Babe Ruth fashion.

She was a beatin' and a whompin' him senseless.

I stupidly thought I was the answer to this problem and grabbed this (much larger than me) lady's bat-wielding arm. Even though I should have known that adrenalin and a misinformed sense of duty, at that moment, all conspired in my being flung over the hood of a car.

Not wanting to be smacked down again, I slapped a set of cuffs on one wrist, barely being able to lock them due to the ... ah ... sturdiness of her build.

There was no way I could get her other arm back as far as needed, so I took John's cuffs as used them as an extender. The situation should have been done but for the fact that I was in the wrong part of town and holding, possibly, one of these (now rapidly multiplying) members' aunt or some kinda' relation which would lead to an even *more* elevated level of ass whippun!

I didn't have long to ponder the situation before John pulled a small .38 caliber revolver from somewhere on his person, pointed it at the largest of the members, shouting a few threatening obscenities while pointing the pistol directly at the young man's nose.

Always, humor has been the great equalizer in my life. Some may call it sarcasm but I like to think of it as a tension diffuser.

"John," I asked. "How many of these young gents do you suppose are here?"

Looking about, as if it would make a difference, he said, "25 or 30?" Now his wheels were starting to turn.

"John, how many bullets does your gun carry?"

"Five," he said, then looked at me, and then at the pistol. Spinning in place, he ran to the ambulance, locked himself in, and got on his radio, still pointing the gun from behind the windows.

I held up the keys, waving them at him to possibly make him come back from the planet he came from and was currently visiting.

The leader looked at me, not with anger anymore, but with what I believe was pity for having this butt-munch as a partner.

Within minutes, we found out who he called on his handy radio: Everyone!

Whatever he said brought a heard of police in all forms: cars, trucks & vans. They were armed fairly well, if you were attacking a fort. Needless to say, the group of T-shirted guys dispersed quite speedily.

I quickly told the captain what was going on.

And even more needless to say, John was in deep. He lost his gun and, later that day, his position. He drove back with the captain in his cruiser.

And that's proof that humor (aka sarcasm) is better than all-out war.

Lets see ... Chicken at the Polk Deli or the late night burger place on Geary and Masonic ... which goes better with Pepsi this time of night?

10/7/ m

TWENTY-THREE
"I'M A 5150!"

There are many Police codes. Their favorite is, as was ours, 10/7/m ... time for food! One that took some more preparing for was '5150'... or "Bring the Net!"

This was reserved for those with a confused sense of path ... or a ... well ... ok, the nutsos.

One always had to be prepared for a smiler, screamer, biter, or worse. They ran the gamut from happy clowns to weapon-wielding full-on crazies.

One cold night, we get the famous 5150 call and are told to be careful as strange noises were emanating from the apartment. Getting downtown and to the scuzzy hotel, we entered, careful not to touch anything 'cause you could almost catch something, there, from just looking at it.

We went up the two-person 70-year old elevator, we squeaking and bouncing all the way up to the fifth floor. That night, I had a new, almost virginal, partner. To the front door he marched with flashlight in hand, went to knock.

I grabbed his hand before it hit, and told him the proper procedure was to knock from an arm's length to the side of the door. But most of all, listen first before doing anything.

We didn't have to strain to hear grunts and noises akin to a badly dubbed Japanese Karate movie. Soon, we'd find out how spot on I was.

He knocked from the side... and instantly, a sword slammed through the door precisely in the spot my young partner had first stood.

I kicked the door open. By that time, our patient had jumped back onto his bed and began to pour those industrial size cans of condiments over himself.

Yep. Mayo, catsup, relish and mustard, all the while happily saying, "I'm a 5150, take me in."

I was figuring this wasn't his first circus and instructed my partner to wipe him off with a convenient broom. We wrapped him in some sheets, strapped his grinning self to our gurney, added a few improvised straps of that old-time super wide, ever stick adhesive tape, the old kind made of, it seemed, canvas and a layer of gummy glue that never really all came off, but could hold a gorilla to a fence post.

At General Hospital, we hosed him off and took him in to Psych. After it was over, my partner sat in my side of the rig and asked me to drive.

I knew why. "Not what you thought it would be?"

He looked at me and shook his head. At that moment, we got a "GSW, Code 3." That's a gunshot wound.

Looking at my partner, I asked, "A little more like it?" He smiled, still shaking a bit.

But a virgin, no more.

74 DAYS OF DRUGS AND SIRENS

TWENTY-FOUR
SOMETIMES YOU JUST DON'T THINK

Down by the piers, in San Fran, were a whole lot of old, tall turn-of-two-centuries-ago fire traps. One fun-filled day brought us to such a building.

Four or five stories, and a flat roof, with a standpipe that brings water up a multi-storied building and acts like a high up fire hydrant.

Up this place was a fireman, on the roof checking for folks in need. The fire was pretty involved, running up the floors so fast and cutting off the path for inside escape.

The heat went up and around the clay pipe and burst it, dropping a large shard on the heel of the fireman, cutting him severely. The news people were below, airing this live.

There was no time to make a normal judgment call. There was a 'pompier ladder' there. Who's, I did not know. But a while back, in fire training, I learned to use this scaling-type ladder to climb on the outside if the building, one story at a time. A length of rope with a climbing harness and I was off ... I mean up!

At the top, I wrapped the fireman's leg with a compression dressing and lowered him over the side. Hooking up, I rappelled down the fiery wall to the loving earth below. At the bottom, I was pretty amped on a caffeine adrenaline super rush to comprehend what had transpired.

An excited newsman pointed to the top of a now-fully-involved building, and stuck a microphone in my face. "Do you *know* what you just did?"

I looked at his hand and continued my gaze up ... up ... up ... and as my head went back to see the height, I just kept going and fell backwards, onto some poor bystanders.

Some thought I fainted. I like to believe I was just over come with amazement.

Awww, hell, I fainted!

TWENTY-FIVE
GHOST RIDER, I AIN'T

Getting around San Francisco in an ambulance is the greatest. Not that any emergency type organization would ever use a siren for say, getting through traffic to get to a restaurant or date or the such. Never!

But, time off is of the essence when the work day can be three in a row. Parking in San Francisco is a horror story. How to cure it? A Motorcycle!

Yeah, that's right. Follow 72 hours straight on duty by hopping on a two-wheeled widow maker! Not like you didn't pick up enough idiots in bike wrecks on duty, let's ride exhausted and half-crazed from physically abusing your body.

One of my patients, who tore himself up on a bike, worked at a finance company. He told me about a bike repossession that happened when some kid's dad gave his ride back because he juiced it up wildly and got a fistful of tickets.

$500 was the special price to me, of this gas speeding two-wheeled demon. I picked it up at the finance company, paid cash in small bills and rolls of quarters, and it was mine.

Six blocks away, I ran out of gas.

I coasted into a station and used the last of the loose change. I tried to start it. No luck.

Kicked it over again and it threw me up about a foot in the air! Deciding I'm not gonna be beaten by a bike, I pumped up the kick starter and stomped down again. This time, I went over the handle bars and onto the asphalt in so much pain, the attendant came out to help the screaming 'Biker' crying on the floor. "Call this number and tell the dispatcher that the paramedic of Crew 111 is down and needs *quiet* help ASAP."

Within minutes, a rig showed up, splinted my foot, rolled the bike into the rig and off we went. Oh, and they gave me two Empirin 4s with codeine, the strong ones. We got to Emergency and the guys got me to a throng of nurses who knew me. They pulled me directly into a room and gave me a couple more Empirin 4s, yes, also with codeine.

While waiting, my 'Dingo Boot' was cut off. It was a great looking boot, but had complete crap support. A tiny nurse, who must have known me, gave me a couple of "pills for pain," as she said. "It will make the hurt go all away."

By this time and pill count, I wouldn't have felt the snapping off of a toe.

A half hour later, with a freshly-wrapped slightly torn Achilles tendon, I was released to my future wife Joanne to take to my apartment.

With her help, we hobbled to my place, from parking and I plopped on the floor in the front room by the fire place. At this exact point, all the codeine met inside my body and started to party. I hallucinated, seeing things running up and down my arms for awhile.

She remained with me till I calmed down and seemed of no danger to myself, others, or the critters running up and down my body.

By the way... my medical record reads, to this day, "No damn Codeine...highly allergic!"

Three days later, dried out and with a walking cast, one of my buds brought over and affixed to me, I was back and on the rig again. Ain't a strong youthful body and insanity great buddies?

Ask me today at 63 years old. ha ha ha, owwww.

Trust Me, I'm a Paramedic

TWENTY-SIX
HOW I MET MY WIFE
OR ... "THE GREAT EXTORTION"

As usual, I got the cardiac calls.

This time to a doctor's office on West Portal in the city, where I ran into one of my regulars, Oris. He was on the floor in the reception area by the front desk, having a helluva time breathing, as he had a pretty good case of chronic congestive heart failure.

Having treated him on several occasions, I proceeded to set up his I.V. and pull out the drug Lasix for an injection into the line as soon as ready.

This cute curly-haired brunette nurse walked out in a spotted blue and white tunic and white-belled pants, looking at me. Being the town playboy (in my mind, anyway), good-lookers never slowed me down.

She stopped me for a long moment. "I'm Mike. Who are you?"

She looked at me as if I just killed a kitten, saying "You need to help him."

"No problem. By the way," as I started the I.V., "When can I take you to dinner?" Needless to say, she was a bit taken aback by her thought of poor timing and my cold, cold nature. Fairly upset, she said something but I was just staring at her. She told me years later I was making her very nervous. "Well?"

"Fix him, this isn't the time." she ordered.

Never really slowing down and endangering my old buddy, I asked her if she knew what medication to give him?

"NO," her response.

"Well I do, and dinner would expedite my remembering which one to give."

Long story short, as it all happened in moments, she agreed to go out with me but to "Just give him the shot!" I was ready anyway and stuck the needle in the tube.

During the entire exchange, Oris was looking back and forth between Joanne and myself, prompting her to answer, and for me to hurry the hell up! For some reason, I pulled the needle out for a split second and asked her, "You're not just saying that so I'll save him, are you?"

Oris said, "No, she Ain't lyin!"

She nodded, I pushed the med and my old patient was much better in a few short minutes.

While packing our gear and Oris, I asked her for her number, she hesitated momentarily then wrote it on a small piece of the doc's note pad, and gave it to me with a curious smile.

Not to ever let cobwebs grow on me, I called her two days later when my shift(s) ended. No answer.

I kept calling, and finally a little over three weeks later, I got her on the phone. She had been up at Lake Shasta with her family and seemed glad to be home and that I called.

Well, can I tell ya? I saw her once and knew I was done in. She asked me if I was like that with everyone on the first meeting?

"Of course! But this was the first time I meant it!"

Must not have scared her off as we were married within a year, and now for 35 and climbing.

TWENTY-SEVEN
HUMOR TRUMPS DRUGS

There are just so many hours you can work an ambulance driver. Obviously, the same rule did not apply to the Paramedic. Now, into the umpteenth hour of a long shift, we'd used up *two ambulances* full of stuff.

Pulling in, after having burned out my drivers, I was ready for a long sleep. As I walked in, a new driver grabbed me, stuffed me into the rig and off we went loudly with pretty lights swirling overhead, across the city to cardiac call

We pulled up in front of a restaurant and I did what I usually did, shot from the ride to the scene of whatever was happening. To my exhausted shock, this rig had not been restocked.

We had nothing. No med kit, drugs or oxygen.

Where the hell did he find this thing? There's always *something* left, not stripped. Well, this was time for some serious creativity. I had a basic I.V. and that was it. So I hooked him up to the monitor and told my partner, "Lets scoot!"

I whispered to him. "No siren, plenty of lights and speed!" In the rig I flipped the switch to run a tape of his heart rate and rhythm.

Oh crap. His read was horrible: premature beats, no regularity and he was starting to get real anxious.

Right then it hit me, and I started to smile and talk to him as if we were friends just joking around. The response I got was what I had hoped for: confusion.

"Are you crazy? I'm having a heart attack here!"

I told him, "What you're having is an anxiety response. By the way, are you Italian, seems so by your last name?"

Now, in a slightly calmer voice, "Yeah...Genovese."

"Oh,' I said. "Gangsters," and smiled really big.

"Yeah, and don't forget it."

I *almost* had him grinning!

I continued with a quick line of all my best Italian jokes till I looked up and we were pulling into the ER. Out, we flew. I verbally gave them my readings.

The ER doc hooked my 3-lead (a minimal set of attachments for monitoring the heart) up to their monitor, listened with the scope, checked nails, lips, eyes for any cyanosis (blue tint because of bad air passing). He checked everything, stopped and turned to me saying, "Are you kidding me?"

There were no immediate signs of having any problems at all, so I thought and said "Wait!" I ran to the rig and scooped up a mile's worth of EKG readout, and handed it to the doc.

He looked hard, then to me and said, "Sorry, but without meds, O2 or anything else ... How?"

"20 minutes of matinee comedy 'shtick' (old time comedy club jokes)." I turned, tipped my head towards the now-calm and smiling patient, then out the door.

Outside, my driver asked me, "Want another run?"

I guess my look said "no" and then he asked "Want me to drop you off home?"

For that run... I was okay.

MICHAEL ROMANO   85

DIRECT FROM B'WAY
NEW SHOW
EVERY MONDAY
CAROL DODA
SINCE 1965
DIRECT FROM B'WAY
NEW SHOW
EVERY MONDAY
WOW!
TASTE THE FORBIDDEN FRUIT
The
TOP XXX HITS
LOOK
CONDOR
THRILLING ADULT PARTY
300 COLUMBUS AVE @ BROADWAY SAN FRANCISCO, CA
—FULLY AIR-CONDITIONED—
UPPER

TWENTY-EIGHT
BOOBS CAN HEAL, REALLY!

One of our standby points was on Columbus street in front of the old Condor Club, where the amazing Carol Doda performed her magic dance and featured her legendary, supernatural breasts.

I sat back in the ambulance, enjoying the lights and gawking tourists. I had just popped the top on my evening libation, a frosty Pepsi, when a call came in.

"Code three cardiac, Condor Club."

I looked at my partner, grabbed the mic' and said "10/97."

"Already?" the radio answered back.

By that time, we were already getting the gurney, packing gear and running to the door. Once inside, the manager led us to the stage area where a well-dressed man was sitting down, looking like hell.

The usual routine: O2, paddles on chest to read till we got the leads on.

Then the very sick man made a surprising declaration: "I'm not leavin' till I see them!"

"See what?" was my response as I started the I.V.

"I came here from Utah and I ain't leavin' till I see them!" The manager looked at me and we both knew he meant Carol's super-sized entertainers.

I told him his EKG was having a fit. "Sir, we have to leave right now!"

He grabbed my wrist. "Not yet!" He looked directly into my eyes with a determination I knew would be difficult to overcome. Suddenly, his expression changed as he looked over my shoulder.

My first thought was that he was starting to cross over, but I looked over my shoulder to see Miss Doda. She was smiling, effervescent, and bouncing as she approached. Yes, *bouncing*!

She leaned over him, and whispered something in his ear. If he was going to Jesus, he was going with a smile! Then, she gently smacked him in the face with her ample charms.

"I'll be damned," was all that came out of my mouth. His heart rate stabilized and the premature contractions stopped. Now 'I' needed to sit down.

"What...what happened?" she asked.

I explained as best I thought I could, that her generous girls had brought him back from the edge. Her boisterous response was "They can heal too!" followed by an infectious laugh.

I just smiled, she kissed him on the forehead and left the bunch of us grinning from ear to ear. Our patient was on the way out the door to our rig for a quick trip to the ER and couldn't have been happier.

A little post script...

About a hundred years later, I was walking with my 16-year old daughter Gina, arm in arm, shopping on Union Street. Off one of the blocks was a lovely cobblestone alley with some boutique shops.

An older woman, dressed in lace and finery, was sitting out front of - how to put this - a "creative lingerie" shop. Holding a lace parasol over her shoulder to block the sun on her pale skin, dressed in fine filigree clothes with an impressive bustier (a corseted with a built in boobie lifter) she raised her arm and shouts, "Michael!"

Looking around, no one else was in sight, so I made the obligatory 'pointing at myself' motion and she got up, beckoned for us to come over and when I was next to her, hugged me. It was Carol!

Both of us had changed a tad, but nothing could mask that grin she had and her voice was unmistakable. "Who's this, your latest?"

"Not exactly, Carol ... She's my second of three!"

She seemed more than a bit surprised.

Didn't know I had such a reputation, let alone one the most famous stripper in San Francisco would have heard of. My daughter Gina and her exchanged smiles and hands, but I wanted to get her out of there before Carol went into anything my memory had repressed, since I had daughters.

With a hand kiss goodbye, and my Gina's arm in mine. we walked away to Carol's saying "Bye, Bye Mike." Guess that was the first time any of my kids figured out I wasn't just always a dad.

Not in the least bit. ha, Ha!

It was really neat that she remembered.

Bye Carol.....

EXOTIC EROTIC
HALLOWEEN BALL
A HALLOWEEN FANTASY EXTRAVAGANZA!
Saturday,
October 27, 1990
CHRIS ISAAK
"Wild at Heart" Soundtrack
SCREAMING
JAY HAWKINS
PSYCHEFUNKAPUS
BUCK NAKED & THE
BARE BOTTOM BOYS
NOBODY FAMOUS
LZ
DJ EDDIE VORTEX
Cabaret Seating
Multimedia Video Lightshow by
San Francisco Lightworks
GINGA BRAZIL
THE DICK TRACY DANCE REVUE
ECSTACY IN MOTION
$5,000
Costume Contest
Cash & Prizes
$500
Miss Exotic Erotic Ball
Contest (Bikini or Lingerie)
Cash & Prizes
$500
Mr. All American Hunk
Contest
Cash & Prizes
EVERYONE IS A STAR AT THE E

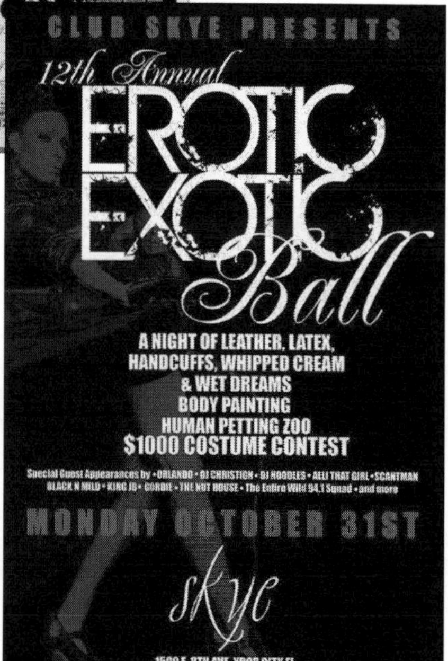
CLUB SKYE PRESENTS
12th Annual
EROTIC
EXOTIC
Ball
A NIGHT OF LEATHER, LATEX,
HANDCUFFS, WHIPPED CREAM
& WET DREAMS
BODY PAINTING
HUMAN PETTING ZOO
$1000 COSTUME CONTEST
Special Guest Appearances by • ORLANDO • DJ CHRISTION • DJ NOODLES • ALLI THAT GIRL • SCANTMAN
BLACK N MILD • KING JB • GORDIE • THE NUT HOUSE • The Entire Wild 94.1 Squad • and more
MONDAY OCTOBER 31ST
skye
1509 E. 8TH AVE. YBOR CITY FL
VIP & BOTTLES: 813.516.SKYE(7593)
WWW.SKYE1509.COM (VISIT WEBSITE FOR PRESALE TICKETS)

TWENTY-NINE
THE EXOTIC EROTIC BALL:
WHAT A GREAT THING TO BEHOLD!

One night a year, the forces all aligned, and thus was born "The Exotic Erotic Ball!" It was sort of where the Sodom and Gomorrah folks went on a Saturday night. The Cloak room had 'Pitch forks, extra appendages, tutus in a size no woman would wear and only a hallucinogenic induced stupor as to what would get left there when it was over.

I was to be the paramedic on duty.

I had been introduced to a plethora of amazing insanities so far ... but this was the Olympics of it all.

First to catch my eye was a couple with clothes everywhere except the good spots. People dressed as their favorite animal. A woman had really good prosthetic extra nipples, well, I think they were prosthetic, with chains and loops connecting them all.

Men and women with piercings connected together with the most beautiful golden chains, some with gems in them.

Every corner of the place seemed like a combination of "That's cool'," "This is a bit different," "What were they thinking?" and "What the hell was that???"

Then, there were the shock value types, the more bizarre the better. It all seemed like a human vegetable soup. Each person added their own taste to the pot.

Oh, yes. Let's not forget the pot!

Then there was me. Dressed as an upstanding citizen of the realm, I felt like a clown at a dinner party, not fitting in at all.

Not having a lot of experience under my belt, in this venue, led to my anxiety as to what to expect and how the hell to treat it.

I finally decided, with the smiles of several under-clad ladies along with a couple thanking me just for being there, giving *them* a feeling of security, to just lighten the heck up and roll along to the rhythm of the ... well, whatever one would call it, sort of an explosion of unbridled fancy.

In fact, I couldn't hide my ear-to-ear grin, but that was partially from the contact high I was getting from the second hand smoke.

Towards the finish, my neck was sore from so much turning and stretching, not to miss a chance to spy something I'd never seen before. Hell...I hadn't seen anything like any of this before.

Finally, at the end, all were sad to go

Me ... damn, I was hungry!

THIRTY
A CLIP OF 32 AUTOMATIC AND
A HUNGRY SAMOAN STOMACH

My new partner was a Filipino guy who knew of a private family party at a restaurant that night and said they were cooking whole pigs!

Next to my favorite liquid intake, all things 'pork' led a mighty hand in making me the man I am today ... and yes, I am currently on Weight Watchers.

Not exactly sure where the location was, I told him to circle the suspected area and my Italian nose would take it from there. One time around and halfway through, I locked onto the aroma of heavenly pig.

Leading us to the door was quite an easy feat for me but impressed the hell out of my driver. Under the pretense of one thing or another, our hosts invited us in, and there it was, my roasted heaven laying there.

"Take all you want!" was the only thing I heard.

We feasted on the great animal, told a few stories to the wonderment of our gracious hosts, and left. As I thanked my partner out front, a very large car pulled up, with even larger gentlemen piling out.

How six of these island beauties even fit in there was for 'Ripley's Believe It or Not!" Three young and (very much) smaller party goers stood their ground in front of the private door.

"We came to have some roast pig," one of the big boys said as he one-armed brushed two of them aside like feathers.

No more than "Hey" was said as one of the young men pulled what later was described as a .32-caliber semi-automatic pistol.

POP, POP! ... and three more times, rang out.

The largest - about 6 foot, 5 inches - and so heavy we couldn't lift him later into the gurney. Didn't really matter cause' the islander palm-smacked the little guy on top of his head and we could hear the crack ten feet away. He dropped like a rock!

I ran over to the shot one and calmed him down, walking him into the front of the rig pressing a large bandage over the spot. But he seemed oddly unaffected. Maybe shock?

My partner put a neck brace on the (now) unconscious one. We back-braced him, then up onto the gurney, in the rig, and off we went. Code two and a half, that's lights, no siren.

We called in a G.S.W. and a probable neck injury with gun shot victim in a good mood, not much apparent pain, just complaining of being hungry. The guy with the neck injury was out like a light with equally responsive pupils and breathing fine.

At the ER, they were split up. I followed the shootee and my partner the now conscious shooter. Doc cleaned up the wounds which bled a surprisingly little.

The patient gently put his large hand on the ER doc and with a kindly voice asked, "Can you please save them for me, I keep them all in a box at home."

The doc said, "Sure, okay with me."

"Thanks," was all the guy responded.

Plucking them out seemed to go quickly and easy.

He may have looked a chunk overweight but that was the most solid overweight I've ever seen. The Doc shook his head in agreement. We left the room for a moment, we felt someone looming over us.

"I'm goin' home now, okay?"

"I advise against it," said the Doc." Hell, you've just been shot!"

"It's okay, doc. Happens more often than you think. Thanks." Then he left into that giant boat mobile and off he went. I looked at the Doc, he just shook his head and walked off.

Me and my partner looked in, then out, grabbed the walkie talkie and said "Back on the air."

Off we went to protect and serve.

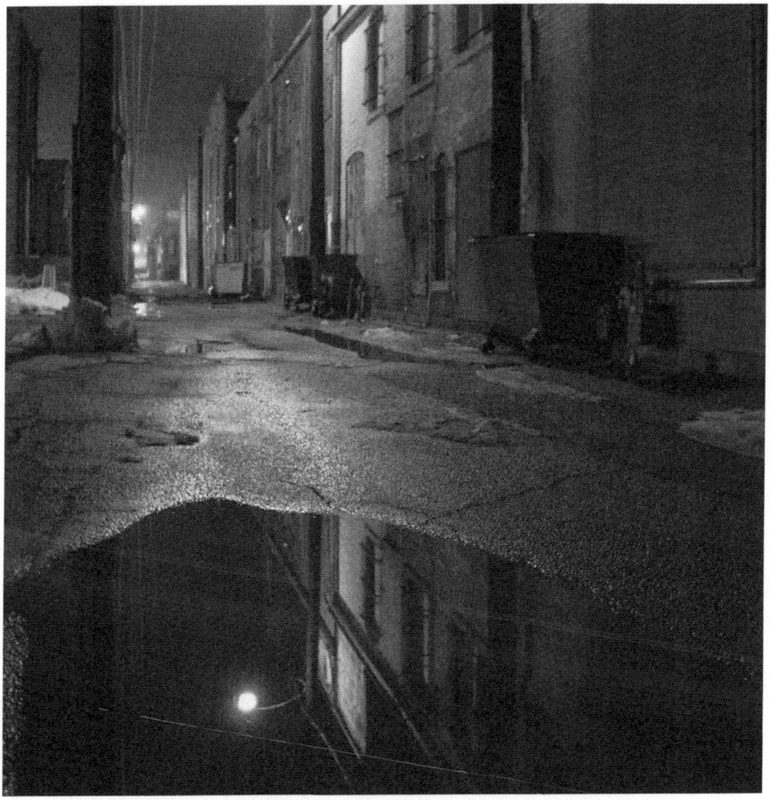

THIRTY-ONE
STOP WHEN YOU HEAR THE CLICK

The setting: an old yellow-lighted alley in Chinatown, me and my partner on a call for someone down. Even before we started down the cobblestoned way, I felt like I was in an old "B" movie.

Suddenly, I hear an ominous CLICK.

Anyone whose has ever chambered a round into a Winchester or any other lever-action rifle can pretty well recognize the sound, especially in an alley in the dead quiet of a dark night.

Placing my arm across my partner, we stopped.

He looked at me in a curious way, thinking, later on he told me, that I was just another paranoid vet who needed some therapy.

"Shhh!" I commanded in whisper.

Still in the shadows, I pushed the gurney hard into the light of that single yellow overhead lamp. The next sound was that of a Winchester shot *through* the gurney!

Both spinning around and taking off in unison, I found myself, even though larger and heavier, running *faster* than my partner, who had the keys to the rig in his hand.

Slowing down, I grabbed him from behind and under his outer arm. I basically carried him at a great clip all the way to the other side of the rig.

After the police came and recovered our gurney, with a clean hole in it, I looked to my buddy as we drove silently off.

"I know," he said. "You need a Pepsi! What the hell is it with you and that can of soda?"

"Perks up the soul, my little friend, and ya' know... so does a good barbequed chicken, so let's get to steppin!"

He shook his head and a little more than that, that night, off we drove in search of a little less excitement.

THIRTY-TWO
C.P.R., A DEAD GUY &
REALLY OLD RUSSIAN LADY RACE DRIVERS

A call for a cardiac arrest and we hit the ground running, out to the older part of SF, where streets have country names, like Russia, etc. The area we were going to have had a good amount of older Russian folks from the way back living there.

Russian little old ladies, well...not always so little, with layered-on clothes. To even get close to the skin in order to put on patches or hear breath sounds meant four or five layers!

At the address, there were the gaggle of obligatory black dressed, by the looks of them, six-layered old ladies. Wringing and clasping their hands and crosses, wailing and frantically waving to us.

We do the drill: park the rig, jump out directly to back, secure gear on gurney, out and at it. We follow the procession up forty stairs and into the bedroom.

The bed contained a very dead old gent. Rigor had already set in. The ladies are screaming and fainting onto various pieces of furniture, and all I could see was a gang of future cardiacs the moment I asked "What were you waiting for before you called me?"

Pops told me to think twice before you speak once, so I whispered to me partner, "Lets start CPR, get him in the gurney, lose them and call it in."

He went onto the gurney, me pumping with one hand, and we went down the stairs, into the rig and off we flew. I kept up compressions while they could see us and thought. "Glad that's over."

Oohh, but it wasn't. Right on our tail were a half-dozen black-garbed hot rod Russian "Omas," staring at me through the back two large windows or the rig. Now, I have to keep up the CPR act until we could shake them!

Speeding, turning sharply, to no avail. Every time I looked up, I could see all of them staring at me through their windshield. Calling ahead to the hospital, we explained our predicament, to the background laughs of the nurses there.

The cardiac nurse asked if I was sure he had expired? I said, "Listen to the crunching!"

Upon arrival, I straddled the "patient" as four paramedics and nurses lifted us out. We really needed to give them a good show to keep them from stroking.

Once in the exam room, with the door shut and no ladies, I sat down for a moment and asked one of the on duty nurses if there was another way out. As we snuck out the side door, we saw the 'Omas' all in pack form, waiting for the doctor to come out.

At least the staff promised to have oxygen on hand and a crash cart.

Sometimes you have to do strange things to slow down the burn, and this was one of those times.

THIRTY-THREE
'I GOTTA' SPLITTING HEADACHE ...AND WHAT'S THAT BUMP IN YOUR HAT?

I always seemed to get the big ones.

Maybe because my dispatchers knew I could handle them ... or I pissed off Mother Nature somewhere along the line and Karma was kicking me in the ass.

To the tall houses in old part of the city, we went. Two and three story, 19th century buildings with high stairs. And as fate would have it, at the very top, was a grand-sized woman with a splitting headache.

I looked at her and was an inch from asking her if she felt good enough to walk. Never having thought this before, I felt almost ashamed for the notion.

Then she laid down on my poor gurney and I swore I could hear it cry.

"Where does the pain start?" I asked.

"Right in the middle of my head top," was exactly how she put it. On her head was one of those stretchy turban hats with a large bump in the center, which I gingerly removed.

To my amazement, was the four-inch handle of an ice pick sticking out from the top of her skull!

"See, I have a headache."

"Yes ma'am ... We're going to get you seen right away."

Down the stairs wasn't as hard as I thought, as I was pretty amazed by the 'Only Headache' complaint.

This was a 'Code Three' as the last time I saw someone with a piece of metal impaled in their head was Vietnam.

The E.R. Doc said, "An Ice Pick?!"

"To the Hilt!" I whispered.

Now in the E.R. and in a room, everybody paraded through to see this. The lady was functioning fine, and except for a heck of a headache, she seemed everyday normal.

We had to leave on another call but came back about eight hours later.

We were told they X-rayed her, sent her to surgery to remove it ... and she was fine, wanting to go home!

Just shaking my head, I walked back to the ambulance. I said to my driver "That's not normal, is it? Oooh, I really need some Chinese food... and a ..."

"Yeah, I know" he said. "I know."

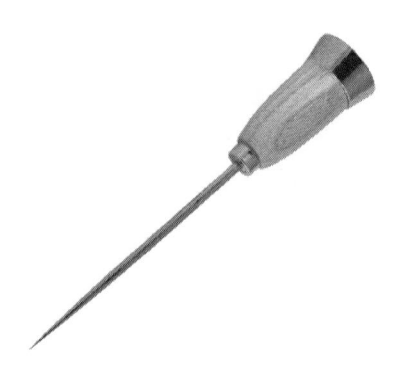

THIRTY-FOUR
STRAIGHT TO HELL, DO NOT PASS GO!

Mary's Help Hospital in Daly City, as it was known years ago, is now called Seton Hospital. Many moons ago, I was coming into the ER with a patient. No great emergency and I was in a spunky mood, so I said "Were 10/7 Our Lady of 280" ... as the hospital sits right off the 280 freeway.

You know how some things just catch on? This one flew across the radios like a wild fire. It was just a harmless little pun way back in the day.

Dial ahead 20 years or so.

I'm in Seton Hospital, walking through the hallways to the X-ray lab to see something of which I can't remember... but I do remember walking right in front of the Statue of Mary and hearing a Paramedic say "10/7 Our Lady of 280."

Then they turned up a hall and I was standing next to a Nun with the same habit as when I was a kid in Catholic school.

She was quite upset, mumbling to herself, rather loudly, "If I ever find out the one who started that 'damnable' name, what I'll say to him!"

I stepped fast away, did a quick sign of the cross and a few prayers, just happy she didn't see the profound guilt on my face and hoping to only get a *little* less time in hell.

Amen.

THIRTY-FIVE
TO A PRIVATE MUSEUM OF AMAZING THINGS

Behind San Francisco General Hospital is the real Crookedest Street anywhere. It's in Potrero Hill, called Vermont street. We found it after dropping off a 5150 at the ER, taking a wrong turn here and there looking for a cold beverage.

At the top we stopped in this nice peaceful wooded area, I snapped the cap and settled down for a good ... minute and a half rest.

"Code Three, Code Blue," a truly nasty call with little or no breathing going on. My driver sets off the lights and siren to the neighbors' delight and punches it towards the hill.

Seeing the first curve before me, my hand was in the upright position, pouring the magic wake me up elixir into my parched throat, he slams on the brake, bringing the butt of the rig about 45 degrees around.

Carefully but quickly traversing the windy way, hitting the sides only. We got to our destination rather rapidly.

It was a little old lady with a sister who, like in my encounter with my future wife, had congestive heart problems. As we pulled up, she was waiting outside.

Putting up her hand to halt us, she looked us both up and down, telling my partner to wait outside as only I should enter.

"Okay, what have we here," I thought.

"Take off your shoes before coming in, please" she kindly asked.

Now ... here is where Kansas ended and Oz began.

Having had a varied upbringing in the arts, I'll have you know, I was greeted by an ancient beautiful painting in an alcove in the foyer.

"This is wonderful, is it very old?" I asked.

"Yes. 10th century on wood."

We entered the living room, white fur rug on the floor, hence the shoeless entry, through a bright, well stuffed living room and into the dining room, a little darker, down the hall to the bedroom door awaiting permission to enter from her sister.

In the few moments I waited, I could recognize I was somewhere out of time. The door opened to an ornately-carved four poster raised bed from the 18th century. Paintings abound and everything looked as if directly from a European museum.

Zip, zip and her sister was right as rain, not quite as bad as she made out. Afterwards, I saw a huge painting on the dining room wall.

"I seem to recognize this one," I told her, "from my mom's old Italian painting books."

"You have very good taste, young man. That's a Michelangelo." I smiled, walked slowly to the front door looking around at such wonderful things, but we had a call and off we went. Not saying anything as I believed them to be either another painters or great copies.

Three weeks, or so, later, we get another call to the same address for the same reason. Everything repeats itself but this time I had a bit of time to talk to her while she showed me around.

The treasures she showed me were of such quality that I stopped talking, stared and just listen to her go on. That night I told Joanne, my lovely wife, about the solid golden 3-foot tall hammered urns, the 17th and 18th century furniture but most of all ... the art.

Michelangelo, Goya, Cimabue and other renowned painters were strewn all over the walls and even one of some super old one in the bathroom! She looked at me and smiled. You guys know *the smile*.

Knowing I never lie to her, mostly out of fear, she figured a lack of sleep made even more intense by a Pepsi overdose gave to my imagination believing this old lady.

Next visit, this was becoming a regular thing, I asked her if I may bring my wife to see these wondrous things as she believes me to have lost a bit of my overtaxed mind. Smiling, she said "Tonight would be fine if alright with you."

Amazed at the ease of that, I jumped at the chance saying an excited "Yes."

Even though she still believed me to be mildly high, she agreed and we were off. At the front door, 7 o'clock and she was out front to greet us with the shoes off before entering request.

In the stark six-by-eight foot foyer was an alcove with a single painting of a superb nature. I turned, first, leading her by the hand onto the huge white bear rug which decorated 'Aladdin's Treasure Trove' which was the front room.

Carved Jade and ivory pieces of large and intricate patterns graced the ornate marble fireplace. To the right, was a solid gold vase almost three feet tall by two feet. Paintings of long-past artists adorned the walls, some with lights illuminating them.

All this pretty well stunned the hell out of my wife. I said, "Wait till you see this." The next room held the largest painting, well the largest one I saw, on the wall, darker as if not as well taken care of, I could still see it was special.

She smiled and flicked a switch, bringing it to life.

The next line she spoke even impressed a young, self absorbed, kid as I was... "This is an unfinished Michelangelo."

At that point I had to ask... "Where, how ... when?"

She was a very simple soul with no real understanding of the worth, *tremendous worth*, of all of these things. Her answer was even more enlightening.

"My husband was an 'Art Curator and Acquirer' in Berlin in the 1940's. We left before the war's end to South America then to San Francisco many years ago."

Then it hit me like a brick. This may have been all stolen loot, but again she said her husband came from a terribly rich family and bought it all.

I was never to know, as that was the last time I ever saw her, her sister or the vast treasure in that humble house. Youth has many gifts, but presence of mind is not always one of them as I simply let it go, never to visit her again. Sometimes... from simple things, spring amazing ones.

THIRTY-SIX
WRONG PLACE, WRONG, WRONG TIME, WRONG SPECIES

Off a long shift, I started to drive home.

I guess my need for food won out over the extreme need to be unconscious, as I found myself off Army street, in the projects. Why the hell I was looking for food there is a puzzle to me unto this day. but there I was, running way overtime on my last Pepsi and waning super fast.

BUMP! SCREAM! THUMP! I stopped my car and ran outside to see what I had hit. A very young German Shepard, although young, still a sizable critter, with a slice in his rear left hock (upper leg) and none-too-happy to let me look at him.

I grabbed my med kit and went back around to see what damage I'd done. By this time, quite a few people had gathered in the street and they were even less happy to see *me* with my car on *their* dog.

The grumbling was getting a bit louder till someone in the growing crowd said "He's one of those 'Paramedics' like on TV. He'll fix him up good!"

Translated: "Please don't kill the guy trying to help."

As if I didn't already have enough to do, now they have total faith that I can work miracles cause they do on TV! Noooo Pressure.

I reached into my pocket for half a Milky Way bar, unwrapped it, and fed it to my pooch patient while I stuck him with a 'Mickey' (calm down shot).

With a disposable razor, I shaved the area to reveal a slash much worse looking than deep but stitches were needed. Steri-Strips were a pretty new thing. Sort of sticky sterile tape and with the aid of a liquid 'Stick' enhancer called 'Tincture of Benzoin' held like super glue.

With a happily candied and supremely calm pup, I proceeded to apply the sutures to close the wound, placing the proper anti-bacterial on it and giving some extra Neosporin and instructions to the (now arrived) owner, on proper care and procedure of our four legged car accident.

Standing up, all I could do was look at the smiling dog, yeah, he was smiling, wipe my face in a job completed, when the crowd started to cheer.

Looking around at all the faces, I could see into them. Pretty neat. I almost got misty, but guys don't do that! Well, not too much.

Back into the instrument of my last event and off home, to bed. Not really that hungry after all.

THIRTY-SEVEN
FELONS, PEOPLE OF TRANSCENDED
SEXUALITY & FEMALES

For a time, I worked as the Prison Medic at 850 Bryant in San Francisco. I was a bit tense being locked into anywhere, let alone with folks who had way more attitude and less than acceptable social skills.

Strangely enough, I took to it right away.

First weekend, I was witness to a pretty evil fight between two young burley ladies of superior musculature and comparable shortness of patience.

I asked the guard why she was standing by and not doing something, and she said, "We're waiting for the Medic to. Oh, here you are! Medics must ask them to stop and check for injuries."

Okay then, lets go...and into the fray I went.

"Ladies, ladies ... lets calm ourselves ... "

I don't think the whole last word got out of my mouth before they were on me, like mountain lions fighting over a piece of meat. Damn, they're strong and know how and where to punch to get their money's worth.

Remembering grade school, "When eminent danger of a nuclear bomb occurs, Drop, Roll & Cover! Well, this was as nuclear as I'd been in, in awhile, so drop, roll, and kept rolling till I found cover.

By this time, four guards were breaking up the ruckus and giggling profusely at the new 'Meat' on the block. That would be me, if you had any doubt.

I smiled back and tipping my hat, and walked strongly back to my desk in the infirmary. Strongly, that is till I was out of sight, then limping and holding several spots on my body that hadn't felt like that since my last motorcycle wreck.

I found that rules seemed to have been suspended here, in a manner, and always kept my guard up.

As I was not sure what they thought of me, but if the first day's "Hello, Ass whippun'" was an indication, I never lead with "Hello Ladies" again.

Yep, I'd arrived and lived to tell about it.

Yeah ... lived ... ouch!

THIRTY-EIGHT
DISCRETION IS THE BETTER PART OF COMPLETELY SCREWING UP

Not everything was flashy and romance, I'll have you know. There were some questionable times, in the beginning, when this new type of 'Uber' ambulance attendant was more a curiosity than an unknown necessity.

For instance, one day, we were called out to aid and assist a dispatch to a commercial fire in a very tall brick building. The flames licked out the windows, up the walls, to the roof.

It seemed like the whole place had fire coming out of every seam. The Captain yelped an order, to the best of my recollection, to put on a tank and breather, go into this fiery hell with another brave soul and search for survivors.

Now, don't get me wrong, fire fighting in one hell of a noble profession due all our respect. But at that very moment, it was not *my* profession and my nobility was seriously in question.

I looked to the Captain asking, "What!"

"You heard me son, step to it, suit up and in!"

"Cap"... My mind was in high gear overdrive now and I said, "If you get injured, who fixes you?"

"You will doc ," he said.

"Now, If *I* get injured ... *then* who will fix you?"

He stared for a beat, reconsidered and turned.

"Gonzales, put on a tank and respirator, you two get in there now."

Although I felt responsible for him, I knew he'd have a way better chance of pulling people out along with himself...a whole lot better than I would!

I gave a sigh of relief saying, "I'll be here ready to take care of anyone you point to sir."

"You'd better be, son" was his response.

In all, two fireman got some pretty ugly burns and several people in the building had serious smoke inhalation.

With my driver and several extra fire fighters helping, we all were able care for everyone on the spot, so as later, they all recovered quickly and completely.

Sure wouldn't have helped for me to go into a fully involved building, get disorientated and end up being carried out on a stretcher, on the eight o'clock news, with my mother watching ... and I know for sure, with soiled underwear.

I'd never get Mom's Spaghetti and Meatball dinner again!

THIRTY-NINE
THAT'S GOTTA BE EMBARRASSING

The combination of dental braces and intimacy oft times go awry. My poor attempt at writing like Shakespeare. Not great huh? Well, we got a Code 2 with a rush and were told to be discreet upon entering. A non-eventful meander throughout the city, a pretty far piece.

Wondered why they pulled me off my area to zoom all the way across San Fran and at 'Code 2." Arrival at the house and things were looking up. One seriously good-looking redhead was standing in the doorway, beckoning to us.

I was liking this big time till I saw the strange look on her face. Sort of a cross between concern and embarrassment. Running up her stairs in my most manly fashion, carrying an oxygen tank and my med kit, she put her hand gingerly, nervously on my shoulder.

"Inside, but just you. And please control yourself and speak as little as possible."

Through the house and into a nice, large bedroom there was someone semi-sitting up against the pillows and a human-looking mound under the covers in front of him a pair of feet sticking out from the bottom of the blankets.

Given her position in his lap, the look on his face should have been more pleasurable than the look of painful concern he had.

"Well, let's see what we have here", as I pulled back the blanket to expose a naked 'heinie' sticking into the air. Immediately, a hand came back and, groping for the covers, yanking them back up over her head!

He explained that she had braces and his skin caught on the rubber band hookey things, he believed.

I pulled my hand down my face to clear my mind and not burst into a horse laugh.

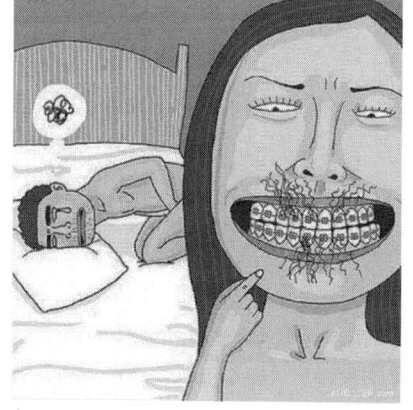

Now I knew why they sent me: years of surgical training ... and this qualified as *delicate* surgery.

Explaining to both how I would do it and "Puleeze' don't jump, twitch or especially bite. With a dental mirror I carried and a really slender hemostat (sort of long slender pliers which these had a curve to), I told them step by step what was going on. Into the gap, I gently clasped the offending skin, stretching it off the attacking brace hook.

When one was free, I said "Ok now..." and she started to get up. He squealed, slammed his head against the back board and she, figuring we weren't totally disconnected, froze.

"Just one more, as far as I can tell, but please don't move till I give the sign" and moved to the other side.

The drool was now starting to really hinder me, so I used a baby aspirator to draw some off.

This was quickly going from humorous to pretty damn disgusting. Got the last chunk in my claw, just as the guy's pleading eyes caught mine.. SNAP!

"Free," I exclaimed!

At which point, the young naked lady sprung up off the bed to who knows where. He grabbed both my shoulders and kept saying, "Thank You man, Thank You."

I just gave a clenched smile, left the house, needing to explain to my partner what I'd been doing so long in there and trying how to explain this over the radio without getting fired or losing my license.

The redhead waved good buy from the doorway, as I slowly pulled away with my hysterically laughing driver. Wonder if she was related to him or her.

Hmmm.

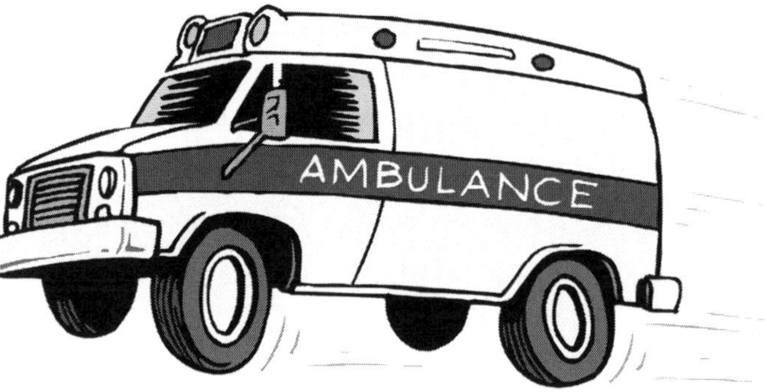
AMBULANCE

FORTY
WHEN FAST JUST AIN'T FAST ENOUGH!

I'm in a "No Tell" hotel with an ancient skinny elevator, my partner, and a belligerent 5150 strapped to gurney. We were all upright when I pushed the button, and the car drops from fifth floor to between 3rd and 2nd, where we were at an angle wedged in the shaft.

We're ringing the bell, our 5150 flailing and cursing, thank God for the straps.

I'm claustrophobic, but believe it or not, within six or seven minutes, the wonderful Fire Department arrived. Guess this was a regular stop. I felt great till one of them said, "We'll have you safely out of there in under half an hour!"

"Back the hell up!" was all I could think of saying.

Putting on my gloves, I coiled myself into a large, mean escaping machine. My partner later said that I revealed a disturbing part of my persona when I battered, punched and cursed my way out of the situation.

I even lifted his lazy butt out of the between-floors elevator. Before I disembarked, I - now calmly - told him to "Kiss my entire ass," to the laughter of the assisting fireman, then walked back to the rig not to speak with him for the remaining hour of my shift.

God....I hate elevators.

FORTY-ONE
SOMETIMES IT AIN'T THE MONEY...

In the way back, ambulance folk (us), were not able to over ride the wishes of the Police or Fire on the scene. Now remember, this was way before either of these esteemed organizations were trained whatsoever in emergency medical care and we were but a handful of ... well, basically, oddities, to be stuffed and tried when or wherever we could fit at the time.

We picked up the sounds of sirens in the vicinity and not being on any call, we moseyed on towards the sound of the guns!

Turning the corner, we saw two fire trucks and a police car, lights flashing, but no one in sight. Into the open door of the house, we could see uniforms out the back door, so we followed. By the pool side was a child lying motionless, two men kneeling by and the mother crying. As we approached asking for an update, we were told the child drowned.

"May I check him out?" I asked.

"He was under for at least ten minutes, he's expired." I was told, "No need to put the mother through any more than necessary."

"Please allow me to try something sir."

The officer looked strangely at me and waved his hand to go ahead. Being winter and the pool so cold, I read children, by their age and response to cold water, may last much longer without breathing than an adult.

We started procedure immediately clearing the airway and artificial respiration.

So fast, the child coughed up a plug of mucous and started to respond, that all around us just went silent. Some oxygen and rubbing of the chest and limbs brought about a rousing crying child to the cheers of all there.

Mom held the boy and we took them to the hospital with a motorcade of fire engines and police cars, more came when they heard over the radio. Pulling into the ER, we had quite a bunch of folks waiting for us.

Mom and son were rushed inside.

As we turned to leave, we stopped in our tracks to see twenty or more fire and police persons waiting for us to emerge.

They started to slowly clap and smile.

What a pay day for all of us, on that cold winter's morning.

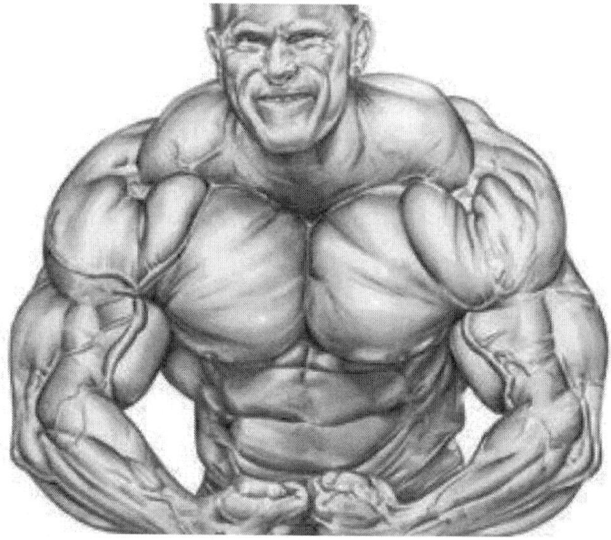

FORTY-TWO
WHEN MEN WERE MEN
AND PAIN MEANT NOTHING!

Climbing up a crazy number of stairs in San Francisco while carrying 90 pounds of equipment, meant nothing to strapping people in their 20's. One time on a call, we had this overly-healthy woman, who had fallen and couldn't get up, comfortably laying on our gurney.

Next step was that we both lift, locking the machine in a high position to roll her to our rig for insertion.

Smooth was the order of the day till just before the insertion into the back of the ambulance, she decided to correct an uncomfortable part and started to wiggle. Only for a second did I turn away to lock the door open and I swear, to this day, I heard the poor gurney cry as it started to fail to hold her up.

Young, stupidly helpful and with not a shred of concern for my future bodily functions, I lunged toward her preventing total collapse and her fall to the pavement. In doing so I was able to, not with any pre-thought whatsoever, get my right forearm between the upper bar and the lower.

Thus, making a clean fracture of my ulna, one of the bones in the arm. To the hospital in a rush code 2, getting help to excise her from the back. Looking around for some help, being quite late, I wandered into the storage room.

Grabbing an arm brace, some roller gauze, I proceeded, with the help of my partner who had now found me, to wrap the affected area.

Damn ... still wiggled and hurt something fierce.

Something caught my eye. A cut piece of lead shielding, used in the X-ray lab to protect your goodies.

I cut a fitting chunk, and with the aid of some wonderful Velcro, used it as an extra wrap brace and protection barrier. It felt great. So much so, I went on a Pepsi induced double shift.

So the shift's now over and a good nap under my belt, I figured I'd best get this arm looked at. Now it had been about three days since the crunch and I was not having any problems so three turned into the better part of a week.

When I took off the lead, wrapping, brace and cotton lining, movement was fine. Then I noticed the lump (that I have to this very day). Went back to the ER, got an x-ray and sat there like one of my patients, waiting. Doc comes out and says, 'Well, if you want a clean heal, we need to possibly break it and reset it plus maybe some greater extent of things may be necessary.

Can't remember exactly what he said after re-break it but I said, "Thanks but no. Gotta go." and off I flew.

Now, that was only one of the many creative and sometimes wonderful abuses I put this God-given self through, and in the immortal words of one of my childhood heroes, Mickey Mantle, if I had known I was gonna live this long, I'd have taken better care of my body!

Well ... amen to that.

FORTY-THREE
WHEN SOMEONE YELLS, "OH SHIT!" AND IS RUNNING BY YOU, FOLLOW QUICKLY AND PASS UP IF YOU CAN!

Deep in the Tenderloin region, which at that time was not you *higher rent district*, shall we say, were some older, possibly under loved hotels. One of those in a prior story had a temperamental elevator.

This lovely four-story establishment had no such amenity, so up the stairs we went, which was okay by me. Dragging up all the equipment as we were told we had someone "down" and in need of some possible cardiac care. Running up four flights with all that gear will tend to slow a person down.

Arriving at the top and met by a local resident, we are informed it was the room waaaaaay down the end of the hall. I hope you remember my penchant towards claustrophobia as I traveled these two and a half foot wide ten foot tall corridors.

I guess the smell and our feet sticking to the carpet with every step, made it a bit less appealing, too. A little more than half way down what seemed to be a hundred yard long causeway, a small, boney, barefoot man lunged through the door shouting "Oh Shit, Oh Shit" over and over again.

As he neared me, all I saw was a large arm coming through the door he'd exited, with what appeared to be an exceptionally large and shiny straight razor in it's hand. Out came the tremendous woman connected to the arm ... and I was off!

I grabbed my partner by the belt and yelled "RUN!"

All I know is I passed up the little barefoot guy at the second floor with my partner close behind, we had just both had 'Life Saving' Pepsis. By that time, someone had called SFPD, and God bless their crazy little selves but they ran right up the stairs.

Then there was a ruckus, a whompin and a stompin was ensuing. Several minutes later, they brought her downstairs, and when I said they, I meant it took *all of them*, even though it took three sets of cuffs to connect her. They asked me to check her over and see if she was stable for transport or needed any immediate attention.

Between her spitting and trying to bite me, I could see she was fit for something anyway. "She seems ok, guys," but you two officers, come to the rig and let me clean those wounds."

Inside the ambulance, the two officers were just shaking their heads. "It's Saturday night, full moon and our shift just started. Just wondering what else is going to pop up before the 'baying' stops."

Holding my hands out to my sides like a carnival barker, I laughed saying, "This is just a prelude to the main event that awaits all in the 'Center Ring!'

They both got it and did their best to muster up a laugh or two.

When all said and done, I never got to where I ever could be completely ready for what was next. I just knew it would not be too boring. No, not at all!

FORTY-FOUR
DEJA VU ALL OVER AGAIN
TO COIN THE GREAT YOGI BERRA

The more I go over things, the more I begin to understand what it took to do the job. From the jump when we started in L.A. we were underfunded and Dr Martin Lewis - I know, sounds like a comedy group from the way back - a great doc and teacher, gave all he had and more.

So well he taught us, that almost at the end of our classes, right there up in front, he went down with a heart attack.

Couldn't have happened to him in a better place. The best of the best, he trained so hard and long, were all over him like a hungry dog on a soup bone.

All the training was so good, that he was back in eight days to see us finish and graduate us with a diploma, a handshake and probably a dirty joke.

But I'm getting too far ahead.

When we all shifted our whole class and studies to Sacramento, "under-funded" would have been an improvement. Three to an apartment and we took part time jobs to put money into the pot to get food.

We even applied for food stamps but the government said, "Paramedics ... Great notion, just what the country needs! Too bad it doesn't qualify, but good luck."

"Well if that ain't the pits," my illustrious roommate said. Not exactly my response, but we'll leave it at that. Doing free time in ERs for training, we were allowed to stock our kits for school.

The ambulance companies we rode along with, also for no pay whatsoever, kicked in goodies for kits too. Stuff we could use for food trade and apartment rent reduction.

Several of us taught swimming on weekends along with artificial respiration. At nights, we had C.P.R. classes for 5.00 a head. Pool came into play for two of us as either we were really as good as we believed...or they stank on ice. Probably just enough of both to give us 40 to 50 bucks a week towards meals.

The butcher loved us as we kept his cut kit and training up to date. We got some free cuts of seriously tough meats, bologna and salami ends, also odd tidbits that smelled ok and we thought it better not to ask.

Buying some older mushrooms and celery with a few of the potatoes with eyes growing, for a greatly reduced price, I could and still can, although with better material now, make the best soup known to people kind.

My secret spices, and my mom's secret recipe for dumplings made for a wonderful giant pot of soup which fed a bunch of us, the poor ones for three meals or better. Mom's legendary spaghetti sauce was always loved, even by the ones who had money.

A pot we found at a garage sale, probably from the army as it took two burners to get it going, was the all-in-one cooking utensil for our mass meal making.

We'd cook soup, pasta sauce ... then the pasta and even stews or whatever we could use it for, as gas was in the rent so we didn't care how much juice it took to heat that behemoth up.

Even so, money was so thin as to take from our study time. I called my mom and brother and told then all was going fine ... but she was an Italian mom and always knew when I was lying, even when I thought I sounded really sincere!

"You have a savings, you know." she said as a matter of fact.

"I spent that the first month, eight months ago, mom."

"No, you didn't. There's your Gerber's Baby Life Insurance policy with a savings of somewhere near eight thousand dollars in it."

As everyone who knows me, I am never at a loss. I was able to respond instantly, but incoherently. "How fast can I get it, Mom?"

My brother told her about two weeks.

Ahead they went.

In the mail, two weeks later, came a check for food for the rest of the run for all of us and then some.

Mom knew I wouldn't ask, but she also believed in what we could mean in the field, and I'd like to believe she felt as much for what we achieved as we did.

I think, wherever our class ended up, we all remember the hardest of times as maybe having been the best.

Doctor Lewis was back on his feet by now and said how proud of us he was for jumping into action so fast. I bet he also was extremely happy that he was one hell of a teacher and we didn't kill him!

Naw, I truly believe he had every confidence in us, allowing him to calmly settle back and let us do our do.

Soon after that, we all went our ways, mine finally ending up in the magnificent 'Three Ring Circus of Oz,' better known as the city of the Golden Gate, San Francisco.

I came here with nothing but a few changes of clothes, less money and a brain splitting with ideas and knowledge, yet unknown to the people doing things never before seen outside of war zones.

The days of splint and run were over. We were here to stay, and we took over with great energy, some curiosity and a lotta knowledge. At the time, we were given full rein to do what was necessary.

We did... and in there lies the stories.

They watched us very carefully, allowed us to help them ... and learned.

FORTY-FIVE
ONE LAST THING

A bunch of years later, I revisited the ambulance company I had spent so much of my being with.

New rigs, new technology and a new 20 foot wide by 8 foot tall electronic map of the city, showing the exact spot each and every ambulance was stationed.

Well, there went all the hiding and hustling. But what struck me the most were all the young faces. Damn, was I ever that young?

Over in the corner I heard my name being bandied about. Curious as hell, I slid on over, unnoticed, to eavesdrop.

Several of them were talking about me as if I were some legend, citing grandiose things I had done and a few may have even been true. Odd, hearing yourself spoken about as if you were another person.

I interrupted, asking if they truly believed these stories about this character and almost got my ass handed to me when two of them turned and told me to tread lightly about things I couldn't possibly know about.

I excused my poor manners and thanked them for setting me straight. Now the person with me there, knew me from the old days.

He looked to me, saying "Why didn't you tell them who you are?

"There's no way I could possibly live up to their stories, and I rather like it that way."

BYE FOR AWHILE

Well ... all good times must, hmmm, not end, just change ... and it was time. There was an old newscaster who used to say that all the news that was fit to print, or something to that aspect.

This is all I can remember, as my wife and son restrict my Pepsi intake and six grandkids use up what remnants of grey matter still firing. But if I can slip away, from time to time, free up an extra Pepsi ... I know that there are plenty of memories just waitin' to be dug up.

Sort of a treasure chest on my shoulders that just needs a bit of excavating. Maybe, after I mail off these pages, I'll steal off with a pencil, pad of paper and a six pack of inspiration ... and really dig deep!

Listen for the sirens. I won't be far behind.

Oops ... there's one now ... See ya!

Phantom 111
Mike
10/97

DEDICATION

From we the first, to you, the many... good job.

Every day I hear stories that make me proud to be sort of, you guys and ladies of the Paramedic corps', Grandfather.

Every one bandies around the name 'Hero'...But I always considered myself as a technician, who never would give up mentally or physically.

I, as I know you, pride yourself on a completed job more than any praise given. Don't get me wrong... I love a good cheer too, but mine own worst critic is my reflection.

I could not have given less than my last breath if I wanted to....and I know this is how you feel.

The drive to excel to your maximum is always in you, so never let anyone tell you it's over till your last erg of strength has left.

May we all be blessed with heart, mind and determination.

You are best of the best...
Thanks....
Grandpa Mike

CREDITS

REMEMBERER: Mike Romano

MY THREE KIDS: Amy, Gina & Josh, who made me do it.

MY WIFE: The same one from the story, and still putting up with me. Thanks, Joanne.

EDITOR: My Buddy & Cruel Word Genius, Dennis Willis

MY SIX GRANDKIDS: Who will know that grandpa, at one time ... was cool and daring ... not this bumbling old fart tickle-torturing them.

AND TO ALL I RODE WITH: Thanks for helping push me to be the best I could have been.

                        111
                        10/7 Out
                         Mike

Printed in Great Britain
by Amazon.co.uk, Ltd.,
Marston Gate.